Kristin Antelman
Editor

T0143582

Database-Driven Web Sites

Database-Driven Web Sites has been co-published simultaneously as *Internet Reference Services Quarterly*, Volume 7, Numbers 1/2 2002.

Pre-publication
REVIEWS,
COMMENTARIES,
EVALUATIONS . . .

The Haworth Information Press
An Imprint of The Haworth Press, Inc.

Database-Driven Web Sites

Database-Driven Web Sites has been co-published simultaneously as *Internet Reference Services Quarterly*, Volume 7, Numbers 1/2 2002.

Internet Reference Services Quarterly Monographic "Separates"

Below is a list of "separates," which in serials librarianship means a special issue simultaneously published as a special journal issue or double-issue and as a "separate" hardbound monograph. (This is a format which we also call a "DocuSerial.")

"Separates" are published because specialized libraries or professionals may wish to purchase a specific thematic issue by itself in a format which can be separately cataloged and shelved, as opposed to purchasing the journal on an on-going basis. Faculty members may also more easily consider a "separate" for classroom adoption.

"Separates" are carefully classified separately with the major book jobbers so that the journal tie-in can be noted on new book order slips to avoid duplicate purchasing.

You may wish to visit Haworth's website at . . .

http://www.HaworthPress.com

. . . to search our online catalog for complete tables of contents of these separates and related publications.

You may also call 1-800-HAWORTH (outside US/Canada: 607-722-5857), or Fax: 1-800-895-0582 (outside US/Canada: 607-771-0012), or e-mail at:

getinfo@haworthpressinc.com

Database-Driven Web Sites, edited by Kristin Antelman, MS (Vol. 7, No. 1/2, 2002). *Profiles numerous successful uses of database-driven content to deliver common library services on the Internet.*

Bioterrorism and Political Violence: Web Resources, edited by M. Sandra Wood, MLS, MBA (Vol. 6, No. 3/4, 2002). *Describes how to find reliable information on bioterrorism via the Internet.*

The Challenge of Internet Literacy: The Instruction-Web Convergence, edited by Lyn Elizabeth M. Martin, BA, MLS (Vol. 2, No. 2/3, 1997). *"A source of valuable advice. . . . Recommended for institutions that collect library science materials on a comprehensive level." (Library & Information Science Annual 1999)*

Database-Driven Web Sites

Kristin Antelman
Editor

Database-Driven Web Sites has been co-published simultaneously as *Internet Reference Services Quarterly*, Volume 7, Numbers 1/2 2002.

The Haworth Information Press
An Imprint of
The Haworth Press, Inc.
New York • London • Oxford

Published by

The Haworth Information Press®, 10 Alice Street, Binghamton, NY 13904-1580 USA

The Haworth Information Press® is an imprint of The Haworth Press, Inc., 10 Alice Street, Binghamton, NY 13904-1580 USA.

Database-Driven Web Sites has been co-published simultaneously as *Internet Reference Services Quarterly*, Volume 7, Numbers 1/2 2002.

The development, preparation, and publication of this work has been undertaken with great care. However, the publisher, employees, editors, and agents of The Haworth Press and all imprints of The Haworth Press, Inc., including The Haworth Medical Press® and Pharmaceutical Products Press®, are not responsible for any errors contained herein or for consequences that may ensue from use of materials or information contained in this work. Opinions expressed by the author(s) are not necessarily those of The Haworth Press, Inc. With regard to case studies, identities and circumstances of individuals discussed herein have been changed to protect confidentiality. Any resemblance to actual persons, living or dead, is entirely coincidental.

Cover design by Jennifer Gaska.

Library of Congress Cataloging-in-Publication Data

Database-driven Web sites / Kristin Antelman, editor.
    p. cm.
    Co-published simultaneously as Internet reference services quarterly, v. 7, nos. 1/2 2002.
    Includes bibliographical references and index.
    ISBN 0-7890-1738-5 (alk. paper) – ISBN 0-7890-1739-3 (pbk.: alk. paper)
    1. Library Web sites–United States–Case studies. 2. Library Web sites–Design. 3. Online databases. 4. Electronic information resource searching. 5. Electronic reference services (Libraries) I. Antelman, Kristin. II. Internet reference services quarterly.
Z674.75.W67D38 2002
025.04–dc21

                                                   2002011522

Indexing, Abstracting & Website/Internet Coverage

This section provides you with a list of major indexing & abstracting services. That is to say, each service began covering this periodical during the year noted in the right column. Most Websites which are listed below have indicated that they will either post, disseminate, compile, archive, cite or alert their own Website users with research-based content from this work. (This list is as current as the copyright date of this publication.)

Abstracting, Website/Indexing Coverage .... Year When Coverage Began

- *Applied Social Sciences Index & Abstracts (ASSIA)*
  (Online: ASSI via Data-Star) (CDRom: ASSIA Plus)
  <www.csa.com>. **1996**

- *BUBL Information Service: An Internet-based Information*
  Service for the UK higher education community
  <URL:http://bubl.ac.uk/>. **1996**

- *CINAHL (Cumulative Index to Nursing & Allied Health*
  Literature), in print, EBSCO, and SilverPlatter,
  Data-Star, and PaperChase. (Support materials
  include Subject Heading List, Database Search
  Guide, and instructional video) <www.cinahl.com>. **1996**

- *CNPIEC Reference Guide: Chinese National Directory*
  of Foreign Periodicals. **1996**

- *Computer Literature Index* **1997**

- *Computing Reviews* **1996**

- *Current Cites [Digital Libraries] [Electronic Publishing]*
  [Multimedia & Hypermedia] [Networks & Networking]
  [General] **1998**

- *Current Index to Journals in Education* **2002**

(continued)

(continued)

Special Bibliographic Notes related to special journal issues
(separates) and indexing/abstracting:

- indexing/abstracting services in this list will also cover material in any "separate" that is co-published simultaneously with Haworth's special thematic journal issue or DocuSerial. Indexing/abstracting usually covers material at the article/chapter level.
- monographic co-editions are intended for either non-subscribers or libraries which intend to purchase a second copy for their circulating collections.
- monographic co-editions are reported to all jobbers/wholesalers/approval plans. The source journal is listed as the "series" to assist the prevention of duplicate purchasing in the same manner utilized for books-in-series.
- to facilitate user/access services all indexing/abstracting services are encouraged to utilize the co-indexing entry note indicated at the bottom of the first page of each article/chapter/contribution.
- this is intended to assist a library user of any reference tool (whether print, electronic, online, or CD-ROM) to locate the monographic version if the library has purchased this version but not a subscription to the source journal.
- individual articles/chapters in any Haworth publication are also available through the Haworth Document Delivery Service (HDDS).

Database-Driven Web Sites

CONTENTS

ABOUT THE EDITOR

Kristin Antelman, MS, is Associate Director for Information Technology at North Carolina State University. She was previously Head of Systems & Networking at the University of Arizona Health Sciences Library. Ms. Antelman is the author of "Getting Out of the HTML Business" (*Informational Technology and Libraries*) and has presented a LITA Regional Institute, "Database-Driven Web Sites," numerous times across the country. She is active in the American Library Association.

Preface:
Unleashing the Potential
of Database-Driven Web Sites

Creating database-driven Web pages is a widespread practice in libraries today. Many of those who haven't yet done it are aware of the need and in the planning stages for implementing a solution. No matter what stage of that process you find yourself–from conceptualizing the need for a database to implementing a second-generation solution–it's likely your experience to date has raised more questions, both technical and non-technical, than you have answers for.

This volume contains contributions that range across a spectrum of complexity: from do-it-yourself solutions to those that require a team. The applications described here use both commercial and open source tools to implement typical library Web services. The focus is not on the technology, however, but rather its utility in solving these problems and helping to advance the library's digital "face," that is, its Web site.

Apart from technology, an equally interesting way to look at these projects is how the tool of database-driven Web content can expand the reach of the library. New services can be created that were either impractical or impossible using static HTML-based Web sites. Examples would be Ogilvie and Jewell's discussion of creating a complex, personalized portal ("Partnering to Build a State Portal: MyCalifornia"), and Frost's project to organize and describe online reference tools for a broad-based collegiate audience ("The Internet Collegiate Reference Collection"). Underhill and Palmer ("Archival Content Anywhere@ Anytime") show how opening up a library's unique special collections

[Haworth co-indexing entry note]: "Preface: Unleashing the Potential of Database-Driven Web Sites." Antelman, Kristin. Co-published simultaneously in *Internet Reference Services Quarterly* (The Haworth Information Press, an imprint of The Haworth Press, Inc.) Vol. 7, No. 1/2, 2002, pp. xv-xvii; and: *Database-Driven Web Sites* (ed: Kristin Antelman) The Haworth Information Press, an imprint of The Haworth Press, Inc., 2002, pp. xiii-xv. Single or multiple copies of this article are available for a fee from The Haworth Document Delivery Service [1-800-HAWORTH, 9:00 a.m. - 5:00 p.m. (EST). E-mail address: getinfo@ haworthpressinc.com].

xiii

materials finds an audience for those materials and creates new opportunities and responsibilities for the library to serve that audience. Koopman ("Bibliographic Citation Management Software for Web Applications") describes advancing opportunities for collaboration outside the library by adopting researchers' own tools in partnering to develop databases.

As delivering Web content from a backend database becomes common practice, an area in which most of us would benefit by devoting some attention is the staff interfaces to those databases. Several contributors to this volume describe functionally advanced interfaces they have developed. Hein and Davis describe the University of Nebraska at Omaha's Research Wizard, the winner of the 2001 Gale Research Award for Excellence in Reference and Adult Services ("The Research Wizard: An Innovative Web Application for Patron Service"). Westra describes the move to a second generation platform–including staff development tools–for HealthLinks, a sophisticated portal to electronic health information resources at the University of Washington Health Sciences Library ("HealthLinks: A ColdFusion Web Application"). Bennett introduces us to an up-and-coming open source tool, Zope, for creating and managing dynamic Web services ("Appalachian State University Libraries' Ask A Librarian: A Reference Service for ASU Students, Faculty, Staff, and Alumni"). Galván-Estrada describes the University of California at San Diego's Sage Project, which includes a suite of powerful staff tools for managing database content ("Moving Towards a User-Centered, Database-Driven Web Site at the UCSD Libraries").

If staff interfaces are an explicit subtheme of this volume, then a more intangible subtheme is the changing role of the OPAC. One reason for the popularity of creating databases outside the integrated library system is the widespread feeling that the OPAC does not do a good job of delivering certain kinds of content (or viewed another way, that Web lists do a better job). The appeal of a single, Web-based list of journals held by the library, as described by Platt ("Databases to the Web: From Static to Dynamic on the Express"), is undeniable and many libraries are choosing to move in that direction. In this sense the Web journal lists, like citation databases before them, are serving as a seamless bridge from the "collection" level–the journal title–to the "item" level, the individual online article. Eventually we will solve the problem of the fragmented and duplicative presentation of the library's collection to our users. It will be interesting to watch the evolution of new applications for these powerful tools over the coming years.

These "home-grown" solutions can be a valuable learning experience for those of us who develop them, our parent organizations, and the profession as a whole. As we take our Web sites in new directions we will take with us what we've learned from creating these applications. We're learning how our users view our digital collections within the larger library context and what kinds of library services they now need. We've also identified key issues related to management of our digital collections and how they differ from managing paper collections. It's been a short decade since we all learned what "Gopher" was and started our journey down this exciting new path; the next decade promises to keep us moving just as fast.

Kristin Antelman

FEATURE ARTICLES

The Research Wizard:
An Innovative Web Application
for Patron Service

Karen K. Hein
Marc W. Davis

SUMMARY. The Research Wizard, a database-driven Web application developed at the University of Nebraska at Omaha's University Library, provides opportunities to offer patron services in new and innovative ways. Running on an open source PHP/MySQL framework known as iDriver, the Wizard delivers customized content via topical keyword access. Library Web site maintenance frustrations have eased with this move to database-backed Web page generation. While service to patrons is more dynamic and responsive, implementation and ongoing development of this tool bring forth challenges and new perspectives for staff in

---

Karen K. Hein is Reference and Electronic Services Librarian and Marc W. Davis is Manager of Support Services, both at University Library, University of Nebraska at Omaha, 6001 Dodge Street, Omaha, NE 68182-0237.

[Haworth co-indexing entry note]: "The Research Wizard: An Innovative Web Application for Patron Service." Hein, Karen K., and Marc W. Davis. Co-published simultaneously in *Internet Reference Services Quarterly* (The Haworth Information Press, an imprint of The Haworth Press, Inc.) Vol. 7, No. 1/2, 2002, pp. 1-18; and: *Database-Driven Web Sites* (ed: Kristin Antelman) The Haworth Information Press, an imprint of The Haworth Press, Inc., 2002, pp. 1-18. Single or multiple copies of this article are available for a fee from The Haworth Document Delivery Service [1-800-HAWORTH, 9:00 a.m. - 5:00 p.m. (EST). E-mail address: getinfo@haworthpressinc.com].

1

the consideration of patron needs as well as in the evolution of the Library's Web presence. *[Article copies available for a fee from The Haworth Document Delivery Service: 1-800-HAWORTH. E-mail address: <getinfo@ haworthpressinc.com> Website: <http://www.HaworthPress.com> © 2002 by The Haworth Press, Inc. All rights reserved.]*

KEYWORDS. Research Wizard, reference services, Web applications, database-driven Web site, PHP, MySQL, Web site design

INTRODUCTION

In recent years, librarians have faced the challenge of providing access to information existing in electronic formats. The initial response to this challenge by the University Library at the University of Nebraska at Omaha (UNO) reflected established methods used by the profession in the context of print resources. Electronic resources were treated as "just another information source," and access was frequently provided based on the "format" of the electronic source or its print predecessor. On hundreds of library Web sites, distinct Web pages existed for electronic databases, electronic journals, the library catalog, recommended Internet sites, and the like. Patrons were expected to correctly select the format of the resource prior to accessing the resource, much as they were expected to select traditional information sources by using the library catalog for monographs, and print indexes or abstracts for journal sources.

However, neither the electronic environment itself nor patrons raised within the electronic environment were amenable to traditional access methods. Convergence in electronic resources–e.g., the appearance of the full-text database accessed through keyword or Boolean searching–meant format-based classifications no longer accurately described the resource. Patrons experienced in Internet searching or in the use of Internet directories, such as Yahoo, found format-based access confusing and cumbersome. Personalization, an attempt to respond interactively to patron behavior, was an early, but not entirely adequate, response to these environmental factors. In addition, the growth in number and scope of electronic sources presented serious maintenance issues for library Web sites attempting to serve as information gateways or portals.

The Research Wizard, a Web application created by UNO's University Library <http://library.unomaha.edu/research/>, was developed as an attempt to solve the problems resulting from changing information sources and changing patron behaviors and expectations. Accessed through keywords or subject hierarchies, a single page provides links to selected electronic indexes and databases, pre-configured library catalog searches, library resources, selected Web sites, and assistance information for nearly 1,300 topics (see Figure 1). Easily created by non-technical librarians and knowledge workers through Web-based forms (see Figures 2 and 3), keyword topics are frequently customized for individual users, class assignments, topics of current interest, or in response to other information requests.

The Research Wizard was recently named the recipient of the 2001 Gale Group Award for Excellence in Reference and Adult Library Services by the Reference User Services Association (RUSA) of the American Library Association (ALA). In this paper, the evolution of the library's attempts to integrate electronic resources into a "Web gateway" for patrons is discussed. This evolution brings focus to responding to patron needs and the fundamental reassessment of how librarians collect and organize information.

HISTORY OF DEVELOPMENT

The Research Wizard went through three stages of development, reflecting three general types of Web applications: static Web pages, simple Web interactions, and complex Web-based database systems.[1] While it did not gain its name until the third stage of development, the components of the application itself–static Web pages–and the environment that led to the elaboration of static pages into a complex application were present from the beginning. This environment can be understood as an interaction with patrons' information-seeking behaviors in electronic media, an ongoing need to develop efficient methods of maintenance and content updates, a desire to respond more effectively to user needs, and can be termed *service effectiveness, maintenance,* and *customization.*

All are tied to a concept central to the modern library's mission, that of service to users. This reflects, as Veldof et al. state, a movement ". . . into a user-centered paradigm where we challenge ourselves on all fronts to create services that are user-focused."[2] A library's Web presence is included not only as one of the "fronts" but also as one of the larger challenges in providing service. If the Web presence is to serve at all, the user must be at the heart of all considerations regarding basic de-

FIGURE 1

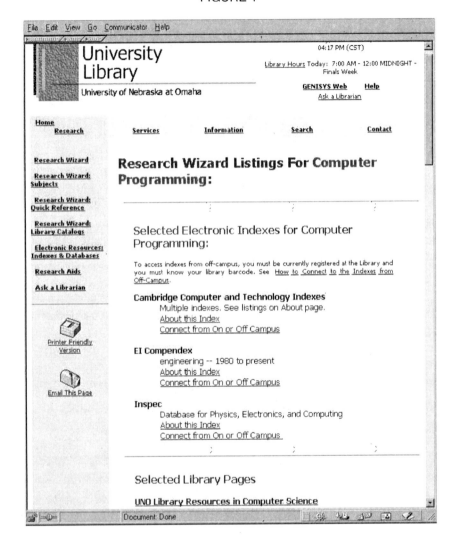

sign and navigation as well as in the development and implementation of tools made accessible through this medium.

 The Research Wizard developed within the library's Web site. In the first edition of the site (1996), access to the library's electronic resources was made available through a single "Electronic Indexes (Databases)" static Web page. In this model, the patron had to know the name

FIGURE 2

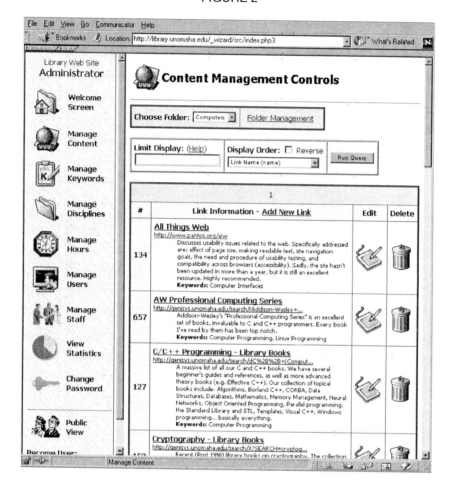

of the provider in order to access a particular index. A secondary access mechanism was through individual "Subject Resources" Web pages. These pages, organized by general subject areas and found outside of the Electronic Indexes (Databases) subsection, contained links to specific print index titles as well as listing other library resources on the topic. Subject Resources pages also included the occasional link to an appropriate Web site. While patrons could access individual databases directly, the challenge was to identify the subject(s) under which a particular index title might be classified. In all cases, the process of con-

FIGURE 3

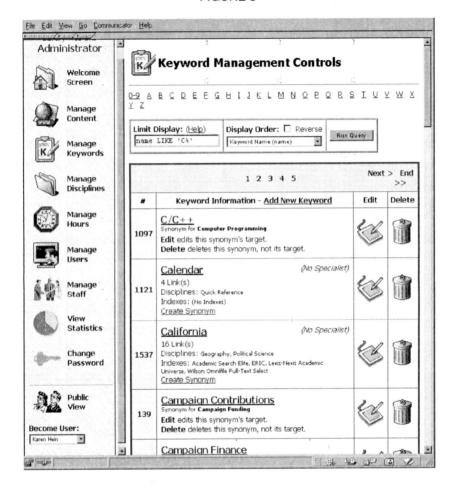

ducting research using electronic resources had the potential for becoming confusing and frustrating. While easily maintained, as there was essentially only one link to each resource, this solution was only minimally effective in providing service and far from customizable.

The second edition of the Web site (1997) brought the first attempts at providing defined subject access to electronic indexes. Modeled after the University of Minnesota's Web site, individual titles were classified into what came to be known as the "Big Six" categories. These categories included: Agriculture, Biology, Ecology, and Health Sciences;

Business and Economics; Fine & Performing Arts, History and Humanities; Government, Law and Political Science; Physical Sciences, Math, Engineering and Computer Science; and Social Sciences and Education. In addition, links to resources were modified so as to provide access to both top-level pages of vendor packages and to individual titles, depending on the database, from the same page and subsection of the Web site. The move to provide more refined links also led to the creation of "About This Index" pages for each link and database title.

Moving to the "Big Six" model, however, did not necessarily alleviate patron frustration in finding an index. While the subject categories were a step forward, the burden was still on the patron to know, first, what subject fit their topic, and second, which resource within these broad categories would be most appropriate to fulfill his/her need. This turned out to be most problematic for those topics and databases considered interdisciplinary or general in nature.

While this solution improved service effectiveness, it gave rise to increasing maintenance issues as development continued. Each database and vendor package listed in the six areas was given its own "About" page in an attempt to further assist patrons in their resource selection decision-making processes. A link to this specialized page would also appear on the Subject Resources page as during this time a standard template for the look and feel of these types of pages was finalized. Included in the template were sections for Indexes (both print and electronic), Internet links and pointers to electronic versions of library-developed handouts and bibliographies, and information for contacting the subject specialist assigned to the topic area.

Developing alongside the Subject Resources pages was a "Quick Reference" subsection. These pages, designed with the intention of capturing answers to the more common or factual questions usually asked at the Reference Desk, also contained links to appropriate electronic indexes and databases and their "About" pages. The proliferation of "About This Index" pages, Subject Resources pages, and Quick Reference pages continued for approximately one year while the next edition of the library's Web site was being prepared.

By the third edition of the library's site (1999), incorporating primarily navigational and cosmetic changes, the number of pages had ballooned to approximately 800, with the largest portion being related to subject access to library resources. Navigation through the Subject Resources and Quick Reference pages, specifically to locate individual databases, became complex, with patrons having to "back out" of subsections and enter others in order to access varying "types" and formats of information tools.

The third edition of the Web site was the penultimate development of the static Web page model. The proliferation of pages and internal links designed to compensate for erratic search behaviors by patrons led to a maintenance "nightmare." A simple change in a database URL, for example, could require the manual editing of dozens of individual pages. It was at this time that a comprehensive plan was formulated to create a single point of access–a Web interface using a database-driven approach to decrease the number of "places" a patron had to look to find resources–and to ease site maintenance complexities arising from duplicated information on growing static HTML Web pages.

Developers gave increasing thought to applying the new architecture and data conceptualizations within the next edition of the library's Web site. Access points and information related to the electronic indexes were initially identified for database conversion. Database access could also be applied to the collected Internet links and library-held materials found in the Subject Resources and Quick Reference pages. Access to all of these resources could be delivered from a single Web page arrived at by a keyword designating a topic area. These more formal classification methods, beyond Big Six categories into individual keywords, would lead patrons to less complicated avenues for locating library resources.

The database framework utilized for transforming links and information was created using PHP/MySQL scripts. This framework came to be known as *iDriver*. Constructed under the open source philosophy, this software provided an application development environment for Web applications, allowing developers to utilize form validation, form creation, and report writing functions without coding each one individually.

The continuing development of the fourth edition of the library's Web site represents ongoing elaboration of these ideas related to database conceptualization. The site went live in July 2000, with an initial list of approximately 1,000 keywords and synonyms available through the section now known as the "Research Wizard." Reference staff worked to match indexes to keyword topics so as to meet a minimal goal of being able to locate appropriate electronic indexes by subject. Adding content (pointers to specific resources) came next. The task of finding and reviewing Internet links as well as other resources within the library in order to add value to the 1,000+ keywords seemed overwhelming at first. Existing Subject Resources and Quick References Web pages were prime candidates for conversion to the Wizard. As mentioned earlier, these pages were already roughly organized by topic and contained links to a variety of resources in various formats.

As staff became more comfortable with the Wizard environment throughout the first year following implementation, efforts moved beyond Subject Resources and Quick Reference pages. The entry of content under individual keywords brought closer scrutiny to the keyword set as a whole. Defining and shaping keyword meanings through content development began to highlight synonymous relationships between keywords and phrases from the initial list. Attempts were made to reflect those relationships by retaining a primary keyword to most accurately describe definition and using the other related phrases/terms as synonyms to serve as secondary access to the primary keyword(s).

Indexes associated with keywords and synonyms were also more deeply reviewed for appropriateness. The goal became to present only the "top" five to seven indexes for that subject rather than presenting all possible resources, even those considered more peripheral to the topic. Subject knowledge and sample searches conducted in the indexes were used to determine a finalized list of resources to be associated with a keyword.

Lastly, contact points through the Research Assistance section were clarified. Reference faculty reviewed the list of keywords and synonyms to determine subject specialist assignment. Subject specialists self-selected those keywords/synonyms with which they preferred to be associated and reflected these choices in the Research Assistance links. As subject assignments shifted within the department, modifications were made to keywords to maintain accuracy.

Service Effectiveness

Today, library staff continues to explore the Research Wizard's capabilities as a uniform, dynamic, and responsive tool. The Wizard provides a single starting point for accessing information by topic, regardless of format. Rather than have a patron visit several places scattered throughout the Library's Web site, the first steps in the research process can be taken by entering a keyword or browsing the topical list of terms. Entering or selecting a specific keyword presents the end user with library staff-selected and recommended electronic indexes (databases), locally held library materials, guides and handouts, and links to other Web resources. In addition, the closing section of the "page" contains information for contacting a subject specialist or the Reference Desk for further research assistance.

Customization

The responsive nature of the Wizard is best captured in the development of specific keywords and accompanying content. As a result of patron inquiries, campus faculty research/teaching needs, and/or the recognition of broader-scale issues facing the library and its user community, library staff members can assemble Wizard pages essentially on-the-fly as needed. Examples include the development of keywords and content for specialized purposes including courses, such as a graduate course in Educational Administration (EDAD9000); particular assignments, e.g., topics such as "eating disorders" or "date rape" assigned to beginning Speech students; or identified groups, including a keyword and related content established for a group of visiting elementary school students from a local community. Recognition of local interests and observances of national events, such as the city of Omaha, the 2000 Presidential Election, and Black History Month, have also been commemorated with Wizard keywords. Dynamic tracking of patron use of the Wizard permits ongoing evaluation of keyword usage and failed attempts, providing insights into patron behavior and needs.

Maintenance

Since the "pages" appearing in response to a user inquiry are entirely generated from multiple databases, maintenance issues have changed significantly. The URL for a database exists only in one place (the "indexes_table" within the Wizard database). Although it might appear on dozens (or hundreds) of keyword pages, the URL can be modified or deleted from all pages with one change to the underlying database table. More importantly, the process of translating content to presentation has been taken out of the hands of a specialized knowledge worker (one who knew HTML or JavaScript and had access to the server) and placed into the hands of reference staff for content development. The staff member can define keywords and synonyms, assign appropriate indexes, include annotated content links, and provide contact information by utilizing browser-based forms. A complete, highly customized keyword page can be created without the use of a word processing program or any coding. As others have noted in developing database-driven Web applications, this "provides an avenue for faculty and library staff to experience the power of the World Wide Web without having to learn HTML."[3] The inclusion of automatic URL verification and testing in the Wizard application insures accuracy in data entry and addresses link-rot issues.

REFERENCE/PUBLIC SERVICE AND OTHER PERSPECTIVES

As work continues in the Wizard environment, the opportunity to review and reflect upon reference service and the role of the librarian presents itself. The largest impact of this tool upon Reference work can be seen in relation to those concepts closely associated with the profession, namely the collection and organization of information in all of its formats and subject expertise. With the Research Wizard, the importance of format and location are lessened. The use of a library is structured, to a degree, by the format or shape in which information appears. Patrons are required to visit particular "spaces" within a building to gather the information they seek. Bound periodicals appear on one floor; book stacks occupy another physical area, with access to either type of resource and the information found within requiring yet another space–possibly a computing workstation or index table. In addition, patrons must know which access tool will lead them to these spaces, i.e., using an electronic database to locate articles in periodicals found on the lower floor or using the OPAC to find library-held materials on their topic.

This is not necessarily a seamless or intuitive process for the patron seeking to conduct comprehensive research, pulling together information from as many resources as possible. The Wizard assists in making the process a bit less daunting in that library staff have recommended appropriate resources, with little consideration for format or location, from a single place (a Web page) accessible by a topical keyword. Shifting the focus of reference service from the format or shape that information takes to a more topical/subject-oriented approach allows for deeper involvement in the real needs of the patron, that of the information itself.

In addition to access tools, library staff at UNO have made an effort to seek and provide pointers to high-quality Web sites of which patrons should be aware as they conduct their research. The Web, regardless of its faults and pitfalls, does contain useful, valid sources of information. Reference work, being closely concerned with evaluating and organizing information for future access, continues to be a necessary support mechanism as patrons encounter the digital world. Providing access through Wizard keywords to Web resources evaluated by library staff is one of the many ways in which patron needs can be met.

The phrase "subject expertise" takes on new meaning with the Research Wizard. Curiosity, personal interest, and/or library school trains library staff members to be information literate individuals. Reference workers learn to employ critical thinking and evaluation skills as resources are reviewed in consideration for inclusion in collections. "On-the-job" experiences and chance encounters also provide opportunities to become acquainted with subject areas in which little or no formal training has been given. All of these past and ongoing experiences can be tapped in the collaborative Wizard environment. No longer does the responsibility for providing appropriate resources on a topic have to rest solely in the hands of one designated "subject specialist." Any staff member can contribute resources for inclusion in the Wizard. This combination of input from varying individuals leads to broader perspectives on topics and, in some cases, a larger number of resource offerings.

The transition to a database-driven approach and the offering of customization and personalization of resources based on subject designation is similar to those enhancements being offered by a variety of others in the networked world. At the time of initial Research Wizard concept development, the trend in Internet sites was to offer personalized views and portals to their constituents. Sites such as MyYahoo, and other My[fill in the blank] home pages, became popular. Libraries also began investigating personalization as North Carolina State University Library and Eric Lease Morgan released MyLibrary to the public. All had an influence on the Research Wizard, though each presented its own issues that influenced Wizard development in taking an altered approach to personalization and customization.

NCSU's MyLibrary offers customization based on a broader definition of a patron—a patron identifies himself/herself based upon preexisting categories defined by MyLibrary creators. While a patron can be presented useful resources in this manner, these items may not always be appropriate, given times when research needs tend towards the interdisciplinary. For example, a patron can identify himself/herself as an "Education major" (student) and be presented with useful resources. This setup assists with the basic needs of the discipline, but it does not necessarily provide the best service to the patron when the "Education major" is researching topics crossing multiple subject perspectives such as Attention Deficit Hyperactivity Disorder (ADHD). For a more comprehensive approach to research in this area, the student may also need to review psychological or medical literature. The self-identified "Education major" would not necessarily have those resources presented on his/her MyLibrary home page because they would be listed under other disciplines not selected.

The Research Wizard, as stated above, takes a slightly different, more fine-grained approach to personalization. Research Wizard keywords and related content can be created for individual patrons, assignments, courses, instructors, or other activities. Pages can be tailored to reflect topics crossing subject "boundaries" as library staff select specific indexes, OPAC searches, and Web links to suit needs. In addition, the patron does not have to log in to the Wizard with a username and password. The customized content is accessible through a single keyword, with the term or phrase being almost anything–a topic, a personal name, a course number, an assignment title, or the like.

In addition to the personalization trend, the Research Wizard reflects changing attitudes of the modern library's purpose. Libraries have traditionally been seen as repositories of recorded information. Recognizing the challenges presented by the ever-expanding Information Age, libraries have moved away from an ideal of being an archive of all knowledge to that of being a gateway to information. The primary underlying concept of the "library as gateway" is that the library assists in meeting information/research needs not by providing the information in and of itself, but by providing well-developed pointers to broader information pathways. The Wizard provides these pointers and paths through keywords and their associated content, giving patrons guided steps and links to resources that may meet their needs.

CHALLENGES

These shifts in perspectives on the location and organization of information and on responsibility and subject expertise have not come easily. It has taken some time to adjust to thinking differently. Moving away from the structure of Library of Congress Subject Headings (LCSH) and controlled vocabularies and into a natural language environment calls for a more patron-centric view when considering keywords and their related content. Getting "inside the minds" of patrons and the context in which topics may be generated poses interesting challenges in collecting and selecting resources specific to a concept. Often, keywords are modified to more accurately reflect the meaning of terms as truly intended or to illustrate particular aspects of specific subjects. Content must then be adjusted to match the more narrowly defined keyword.

Primary examples of these needs are the keyword "Awards" and the distinguishing of "Testing" from "Evaluation" (assessment). "Awards" is an extremely broad category. To lead patrons to more appropriate content, the keyword was split into "Awards" and "Awards–Children's Literature." Links to resources on Nobel Prize and Pulitzer Prize Winners are found under the generic "Awards" while links to Web sites including the Newbery Medal and the Coretta Scott King Award for children's literature are found in "Awards–Children's Literature." In the case of "Testing" and "Evaluation," context comes into play. Patrons with an educational background bring the perspective of using tests and testing as tools to accomplish evaluation and assessment. A more generic definition of testing encompasses topics such as examinations and instruments not necessarily related to the field of education. In order to more clearly define keyword intention, links to tools such as the Graduate Record Exam (GRE) or the Law School Admission Test (LSAT) are provided under "Testing" whereas links to resources for educators looking for information on program assessment and the like are given under "Evaluation."

In addition to term/phrase definitions, it is a challenge to keep up with keyword development in striving to meet patron needs. The initial keyword list was developed from a library staff perspective, representing topics with which staff were already familiar and comfortable. Terms and phrases were taken from already-established Subject Resources and Quick Reference Web pages. Thesauri for various print and electronic indexes were also consulted to identify other keywords for inclusion. This was the case particularly for social science and physical science topics where the final initial keyword list included such terms and phrases as "bryophytes," "desalination," "executive agencies," "fishery sciences," "historical research," "nitrosamines," and "symbiosis." In hindsight, some of these keywords and others seem esoteric and are better suited for graduate students and professors. Being in a metropolitan university setting, however, the focus on this type of academic endeavor is not as intense as one would find elsewhere. The library's main user community is the undergraduate population, and their needs tend towards more basic research activities such as brief assignments and term papers. As a result, specialized keywords such as those listed above have been deleted or refined. Current efforts address a broader, more basic spectrum of topics for beginning researchers while striking a balance with the needs of more advanced users.

The process for developing keywords has undergone refinement to ensure more responsive service. Statistical reports based on failed Wizard queries and queries resulting in multiple hits have greatly assisted staff members in identifying keywords in need of development or attention. Content for keywords such as "abortion," "racism," and "stress management" has been developed after the number of "No Results" (failed hits) reaches a significant number. Classroom instructional sessions also provide insights into other topics being researched by students. "Stumbling" upon undeveloped keywords serves as an additional impetus for gathering content to meet immediate needs.

As alluded to earlier, the idea of a single "subject specialist" is somewhat diminished in the Wizard. Any staff member can generate content for inclusion in the Wizard, and a page retrieved by a keyword query may reflect these varied contributors. No longer can an individual claim complete "ownership" of a keyword/subject area and its content. Allowing others to participate in such a territorial arena as subject specialties requires the development of strong trusting partnerships with colleagues, particularly with closely held topics.

This shift to a more collaborative, generalist, and interdisciplinary environment reflects trends seen in the profession. Reference librarians are finding themselves having to be generalists as libraries stretch to maintain services with static or declining budgets. In addition, the explosion of information brings professionals in the field to a point where it is extremely difficult to be knowledgeable about every single aspect of a subject area.

Combating the notion that research is being made "too easy" by presenting so many resources up-front via a Wizard page is an ever-present challenge. Many initially voiced the opinion that the Research Wizard delivers too much to the researcher, who now appears to be a more passive participant in the research process. While patrons are led to recommended resources, there is still a need for active involvement on the part of the patron. Resources are suggested as starting points from which the patron can explore topics. The intention is to facilitate deeper consideration of the information need and to begin to introduce patrons to useful resources. It is still left to the patron to apply critical thinking skills in reviewing the information retrieved in order to evaluate its relevance to the need. The Wizard, through its single page access, subtly directs patrons to consider all of the various types of resources available when conducting comprehensive research.

FUTURE

The current focus of activity in the Research Wizard is on stabilizing and becoming more comfortable with the entry process and with the Wizard's uncharted capabilities. With work continuing in this environment, glimpses into the future development of this tool can be seen. Currently available as open source software from <http://apocalypse. unomaha.edu/idriver/>, *iDriver* provides an extremely flexible base from which enhancements to both the patron and editor side of the Research Wizard can be made. The ever-changing reference environment has already led to the need for utilities that would aid in the administration of the Wizard. Transitions in departmental staffing create situations not anticipated during initial development phases.

As content is associated with an individual under that individual's account, the need has arisen to create a utility enabling the identification of link (content) owner(s) for a given keyword. Link ownership, once known, can then be transferred to another individual's account when the original owner is no longer available or when subject specialties are reassigned within the department. Currently, the utility developed to handle these situations is still under development and not included in the *iDriver* framework.

Continuous evaluation of the Wizard system as well as additional Web development outside of this tool allows for further exploration of database-driven Web applications and their possibilities. Ideas are beginning to form as lessons are learned and new issues are addressed in the Wizard environment. Many of these are a direct result of the shifting of perspectives mentioned above. It is difficult to articulate exactly how these ideas will manifest themselves into the Research Wizard, though there do appear to be two main themes. These include presentation and/or organization of the content appearing on a page and a more integrated and transparent editor package tying many of the other newly developed Web applications more closely to the Research Wizard.

The future of the Wizard as it relates to public service, reference work in particular, is expansive. Transformation of existing services to patrons will come with innovations on the technical side as described above as well as from the evolution of what it means to be a "reference librarian" in an electronic environment. Exploration of the Wizard as a tool in library instruction and distance education services opens new possibilities for enhancing these services. The number of individuals involved in development and service will increase as more editors outside of the library are sought. There is great opportunity for collaboration with campus faculty in enhancing the student learning experience through the Wizard. Lastly, there are partnership prospects beyond the campus border to be considered.

CONCLUSION

At UNO's University Library, the search for an effective method of responding to a particular population's information-seeking needs and behaviors led to the creation of an integrated, user-oriented Web application that is highly customizable and responsive. Despite the customization and personalization of the presentation, the task of selection has remained firmly in the hands of information professionals rather than being given to either the user him-/herself or to third parties. It is expected that the Research Wizard, or its successors, will continue the trends of integration, customization, and personalization that can be seen in the electronic environment in general. By focusing upon specific user populations, rather than by attempting to be "all things to all people," the Library's continued relevance and central role in the university is ensured. In addition, concentrating on ease of maintenance and the provision of tools to information specialists, rather than on the maintenance and presentation of the content itself, permits those who know to easily and efficiently communicate and share their knowledge in service to the Library's users.

NOTES

1. Jim Q. Chen, "Building Web Applications," *Information Systems Management* 18, no. 1 (Winter 2001): 68.
2. Jerilyn R. Veldof, Michale J. Prasser, and Victoria A. Mills, "Chauffeured by the User: Usability in the Electronic Library," *Journal of Library Administration* 26, no. 3/4 (1999): 116.
3. Paul T. Adalian, Jr., and Judy Swanson, "Locally Developed Web-Enabled Databases: New Roles and Opportunities for Libraries," *Reference Services Review* 29, no. 3 (2001): 239.

WORKS CONSULTED

Adalian, Jr., Paul T., and Judy Swanson. "Locally Developed Web-Enabled Databases: New Roles and Opportunities for Libraries." *Reference Services Review* 29, no. 3 (2001): 238-252.
Antelman, Kristin. "Getting Out of the HTML Business: The Database-Driven Web Site Solution." *Information Technology and Libraries* 18, no. 1 (December 1999):

176-181. Available: <http://www.lita.org/ital/1804_antelman.html>. Accessed: October 23, 2001.

Chen, Jim Q. "Building Web Applications." *Information Systems Management* 18, no. 1 (Winter 2001): 68-80.

Ghaphery, Jimmy, and Dan Ream. "VCU's My Library: Librarians Love It . . . Users? Well, Maybe." *Information Technology and Libraries* 19, no. 4 (2001): 186-190. Available: <http://www.lita.org/ital/1904_ghaphery.html>. Accessed: October 5, 2001.

Morgan, Eric Lease. "MyLibrary in Your Library Could Make for Satisfied Patrons." *Computers in Libraries* 18, no. 5 (May 1998): 40-41.

Tenopir, Carol, and Lisa Ennis. "The Impact of Digital Reference on Librarians and Library Users." *Online* 22, no. 6 (November 1998): 84-87. Available: <http://www.onlineinc.com/onlinemag/OL1998/tenopir11.html>. Accessed: October 23, 2001.

Veldof, Jerilyn R., Michale J. Prasser, and Victoria A. Mills. "Chauffeured by the User: Usability in the Electronic Library." *Journal of Library Administration* 26, no. 3/4 (1999): 115-140.

Winter, Ken. " 'MyLibrary' Can Help Your Library." *American Libraries* 30, no. 7 (August 1999): 65-67.

Archival Content Anywhere@Anytime

Karen J. Underhill
Bruce Palmer

SUMMARY. As many librarians are beginning to acknowledge, the most enduring legacy an institution has to offer the world is its original or unique materials. Digital applications allow the distribution of content on a scale unthinkable a decade ago. The Northern Arizona University Cline Library leapt into the digital fray in 1995 with a pilot Web-based imaging database project <http://www.nau.edu/library/speccoll/imagedb.html>, drawn from a collection of 750,000 historic photographs. Cline Library staff have now turned their attention to the development of a content-driven database that will provide public Internet access to all archival material held at NAU. This article describes the benefits of such a robust tool and the challenges associated with melding archival practice, reference services, and available technology. *[Article copies available for a fee from The Haworth Document Delivery Service: 1-800-HAWORTH. E-mail address: <getinfo@haworthpressinc.com> Website: <http://www.HaworthPress.com> © 2002 by The Haworth Press, Inc. All rights reserved.]*

KEYWORDS. Archives, manuscripts, photographs, users, digitization, database, search engine, reference services

Karen J. Underhill (karen.underhill@nau.edu) is Head of Special Collections and Archives and Bruce Palmer (bruce.palmer@nau.edu) is Head of Library Technology Services, both at Northern Arizona University (NAU) Cline Library, Box 6022, Flagstaff, AZ 86011-6022.

[Haworth co-indexing entry note]: "Archival Content Anywhere@Anytime." Underhill, Karen J., and Bruce Palmer. Co-published simultaneously in *Internet Reference Services Quarterly* (The Haworth Information Press, an imprint of The Haworth Press, Inc.) Vol. 7, No. 1/2, 2002, pp. 19-30; and: *Database-Driven Web Sites* (ed: Kristin Antelman) The Haworth Information Press, an imprint of The Haworth Press, Inc., 2002, pp. 19-30. Single or multiple copies of this article are available for a fee from The Haworth Document Delivery Service [1-800-HAWORTH, 9:00 a.m. - 5:00 p.m. (EST). E-mail address: getinfo@haworthpressinc.com].

19

INTRODUCTION

One beautiful spring day in 1994, Jean Collins, Dean and University Librarian at Northern Arizona University, sat on an outdoor bench with the Head of Special Collections and Archives discussing the possibilities of a new digital world. She turned and said, "Can you pull off a digital project for $50,000?" "Sure," replied the department head, who knew very little about digitization at the time. The goal was simple: work with faculty to establish a database of digitized original photographs, manuscripts, and maps in support of distance education. The Dean's vision, as usual, was somewhat ahead of the curve. She imagined the creation of a full service digital archives to provide access to the treasures housed in Special Collections, anywhere, anytime.

The Cline Library database <http://www.nau.edu/library/speccoll/imagedb.html>, made public in 1995, exceeded expectations; the development process offered numerous learning opportunities.[1] At present, library staff are building upon the success of the initial project by designing a tool that will unite users with a diverse array of content–digital archival objects–in a single click. The benefits and challenges of NAU's digital initiatives will likely resonate with librarians involved in navigating, interpreting, and improving the Internet.

SHIFTING ENVIRONMENT

As Meg Bellinger, the President of OCLC Preservation Resources, has observed, "digital collections are bursting onto the information landscape at a breathtaking pace." Current digital archives undertakings in the United States fall into two broad categories: descriptive databases and content databases. The former type of electronic offering involves finding aids, which are detailed inventories, indexes, or guides to the collections held by an archives, library, or museum. Access to finding aids allows scholars to determine if a collection will satisfy research needs. Most repositories are employing the Encoded Archival Description (EAD) standard and SGML/XML document type definition to encode finding aids. Impressive examples of descriptive databases include the Online Archive of California <oac.cdlib.org> with 5,000+ finding aids and the Bentley Historical Library at the University of Michigan <umich.edu/~bhl/EAD> with 350 guides online.[2]

While some archivists remain adamant that a descriptive framework must be in place before tackling digitization of content, other institutions are making digital surrogates–and accompanying descriptions–available as time and money permit. Perhaps the best known content database, the American Memory project at the Library of Congress <http://memory.loc.gov> serves as a "gateway to rich primary materials [over 7 million digital objects] relating to the history and culture of the United States." Users can explore 2.2 million documents, images, and maps through the Library of Virginia's Digital Library Program <http://lva.lib.va.us/dlp> or a third of a terabyte of digital imagery at the Cornell Digital Library Collections <http://cdl.library.cornell.edu>. Duke University has expanded the capabilities of digital archives by developing the Scriptorium <http://scriptorium.lib.duke.edu/scriptorium>: "a place where texts and images will be created, studied, copied, enhanced. Perhaps one can think of networked multimedia as the modern illuminated manuscript. . . ."[3]

SCOPE OF NAU SPECIAL COLLECTIONS AND ARCHIVES

The mission of the Cline Library, Special Collections and Archives Department is to collect, preserve, and disseminate archival material which documents the history and development of the Colorado Plateau, from prehistory to the present. Interdisciplinary in nature, the collections consist of seven million manuscripts, 750,000 photographs, 950 oral histories, 35,000 books, and 2,000 maps. The department also serves as the home for the University Archives and the holdings of the Arizona Historical Society/Northern Division. A World Wide Web site <www.nau.edu/library/speccoll> allows access to a sampling of these holdings in the form of the image database, finding guides, and exhibits.[4]

Reference services include: 48 hours of onsite operation per week, individual consultation, e-mail, telephone, fax, and mail. Departmental staff will conduct 30 minutes or more of free research for any patron on any topic related to the aforementioned collecting scope. Staff refer users in need of time-intensive assistance to local professional researchers, available for hire. Special Collections handles a heavy volume of requests to duplicate historic images in both traditional and digital formats. Staff routinely negotiate licensing agreements for commercial use of archival material. Onsite visitation averages 5,500 students, faculty, and members of the public per year. The Web site receives 50,000+ "hits" per month. (See Figures 1 and 2.)

FIGURE 1

Northern Arizona University> Cline Library> Special Collections & Archives> Cline Library Image Database> **Record Display**

Retrieved: 10

Search Results - Navajo women weavers   [NEXT 10 RECORDS]

Click on photo or title to view the image description

1: [Navajo woman, dressed in traditional post-Bosque Redondo style, weaving a rug] - Unidentified

2: [Navajo woman, sitting under a summer-style ramada, weaving a rug. A standard-style rug is on display next to her] - F. H. Maude

FIGURE 2

Northern Arizona University> Cline Library> Special Collections & Archives> Cline Library Image Database> **Record Display**

	Order This Photograph For:	
	Personal Use:	**Commercial Use:**
	(please read our copying and reproduction prices before continuing)	(please read our agreements for copying and reproduction and use fee schedules before continuing)
[Navajo woman, dressed in traditional post-Bosque-Redondo style, weaving a rug]	Continue	Continue

Local call number
    NAU PH 246
Creator
    Unidentified
Title
    [Navajo woman, dressed in traditional post-Bosque Redondo style, weaving a rug]
Physical description
    Black-and-white photograph, 16 x 11.5 cm.
Use
    Reproduction requires permission of the repository.
Original creation date
    ca. 1930

Subjects

DIGITAL DATABASE ARCHITECTURE

The Cline Library Image Database runs from a Microsoft Access database stored on a Microsoft Internet Information Server (IIS). Users browse photographers, subjects (Library of Congress Subject Headings), collections, and place names via Web page search templates constructed in ColdFusion Markup Language (CFML); simple queries can be created for image title, photographer, subject, and collection name. Structured Query Language (SQL) commands are embedded in the ColdFusion templates. The existing database does not offer Boolean search capability. Each browse or query retrieves thumbnail JPG images (150 pixels wide) stored on the Library's Web server. These thumbnail images are wrapped with descriptive data from the Access database to assist the user in evaluating the image. A full JPG image (360 pixels high) is linked from the thumbnail as well as from the title of the photograph. Derived from an archival TIFF image scanned at 600 dpi, both thumbnail and full JPG images are set to 72 dpi. TIFF images are all archived to CD-ROM. Descriptive data, originally constructed from MARC variable field elements (e.g., 100-author, 245-title, etc.), have been adapted to the Dublin Core's equivalent elements. Coded with CFML, navigational links within the descriptive data enable vertical and horizontal navigation throughout the database. For example, a user who discovers a photograph taken in Winslow, Arizona can explore other photographs taken in Winslow by simply clicking on the link for "Winslow (Ariz.)" under the "Places" descriptive element.

The knowledge and experience gained from developing the current version of the Image Database guides the Library in plans for enhancement and expansion of the database. As efforts are focused on digital access to a broader range of archival resources through a uniform storage, search, and retrieval application, the complexity of tasks associated with analyzing data structures, identifying digital file types, and developing user-centered interfaces is compounded. Each archival resource type (e.g., letters, maps, photographs, films, or audio/video recorded oral histories) possesses unique characteristics that must be considered in descriptive elements, query protocols, and display formats, to name just a few of the components involved in the design of a functional discovery application.

The production and presentation of metadata directly linked to content forms the core of this discovery application, and the effectiveness of these metadata must be measured against a user's ability to successfully discover and interact with digital content that serves his or her needs. In addition to handling the physical and contextual characteristics of a variety of resource types, the metadata structures established for the NAU discovery application must allow varying levels of specificity in description; the structures must support both item and group level descriptions. To address this requirement, the Library is leveraging the standard complement of 15 Dublin Core (DC)[5] elements–with local elements yet to be identified–for item level descriptions. Staff will employ an adapted Encoded Archival Description (EAD) for group (or collection) level descriptions. Extensible Markup Language (XML) and associated tools will serve as a "unifying" technology for integrating these descriptive elements for presentation.

To accommodate an increasing number of resource types and more sophisticated data structures, the Library is turning to the NAU campus Oracle database installation. Oracle will provide a rich and robust development and production environment for work with data structures, XML, and Web presentation. Planned enhancements for the next generation of the digital resource discovery application include Boolean searching, browsing, and sorting by various data elements (e.g., resource type, date).

BENEFITS

Going digital has resulted in numerous benefits to the Cline Library and its patrons, some intended and some unanticipated. Clearly, a 24/7 environment allows for multiple concurrent users and multiple uses of unique materials. Reviewing access statistics and discovering an audience in places as diverse as Estonia and Taiwan, or the large number of night owl surfers, still thrills the staff. Many digital patrons–especially those who come to the site through a serendipitous Web search–enjoy the opportunity to explore the database in an unmediated fashion.[6] Soon, online ordering of reproductions via interactive forms and imaging on request will increase self-sufficiency. As for preservation, the ability to browse historic photographs in the virtual world has decreased the frequency with which the originals are handled. Although originals are irreplaceable, the replication of images on a server and on CD-ROMs stored off-site promises some recovery from a disaster.

The Library remains pleasantly surprised by the enhanced visibility associated with the database. In 1995, the Berkeley Digital Library SunSITE described the Cline Library's database as "an excellent example of a Web-accessible image database, with full bibliographic records and thumbnail images that link to full-size images." The Scout Report for Social Sciences also gave a favorable review to the image database.[7]

Where once Flagstaff may have been geographically isolated, the Internet has forged new connections. The Library participates in two digital partnerships at present: "Voices of the Colorado Plateau," an online exhibit of oral histories and images drawn from nine regional libraries and museums, and the Arizona Archives Online Project, a collaborative EAD effort to facilitate centralized searching of finding aids for the three state universities and the state archives.[8] Last, but not least, communication with digital patrons frequently enables staff to identify unknown individuals or places in photographs and to engage in collection development as leads surface for possible donations of new material.

JUST DIGITIZE IT (WHY IT ISN'T THAT EASY)

With over seven million archival items to choose from, the staff sometimes feels like a mosquito at a nudist colony–the mosquito knows what is expected but does not know where to begin! By default, the material selected for the digitization will become heavily used. NAU's selection criteria include: research value, frequency of past use, immediate patron need, donor commitments, collection size, financial implications, relevance to the Library's mission, and uniqueness. Difficult decisions arise. Should the Library digitize older collections first? Should project staff digitize whole collections one at a time or select the "gems" from many collections? The answer is a standard one in the archival community: it depends.

Digitization is a labor-intensive, expensive activity. NAU staff estimate that preparation of a simple, single image for the Imaging Database requires at minimum 30 minutes for scanning, file creation, item description, data entry, and quality review. Researching an item to provide context for the user takes longer. Digitizing an oversize map or blueprint or a series of handwritten letters may consume as much as 40 hours of staff time. Perhaps most telling, Steven Puglia, of the National Archives and Records Administration, determined in 1999 that the average cost for digitizing and creating metadata for a mixed format collection is $24.45 per item.[9]

Many archival repositories have turned to outsourcing digitization for large-scale production. The Library of Congress, for example, awarded a multiyear contract in 1998 to JJT, Inc. As one might expect, good communication between the vendor and client is paramount.[10] Academic libraries, such as Carnegie Mellon University and the University of Michigan, have reduced costs by engaging companies that subcontract tasks to vendors overseas. Will watchdog groups on the prowl for evidence of unfair labor issues turn their attention to libraries?

Although archival institutions rarely profit financially from building a digital database, administrators need to be cognizant of the potential for sweatshop conditions.[11]

In the digital environment, the ease of duplication, of alteration, of mass distribution, and of distorting evidence of ownership force archivists to confront old problems–namely copyright, privacy, and cultural sensitivity–in a new light. Until now, the Cline Library has avoided digitizing items for which it does not hold copyright or which are not in the public domain. With the implementation of imaging on request, staff will need to make a good faith effort to locate and secure permission from copyright holders prior to digitizing. Archivists also find themselves on the horns of a dilemma. Digital databases are about "free" access on a global scale for public enlightenment and enjoyment, yet most archival repositories must also function as owners of original items and accompanying copyright by charging royalties or commercial use fees and by preventing loss of control of an item.[12]

When a family donated Grandma's love letters to an archives 10 years ago, did they anticipate how they might react if thousands of people read the letters online? What of Grandma's suitors? Privacy concerns routinely emerge with photographs and motion pictures, usually captured without model releases. Although the Cline Library errs on the side of access, a victim of a violent crime recently asked to have her image removed from the database for personal security. The Library honored her request. Another twist on privacy involves culturally sensitive materials, such as Hopi Snake Dance photos. NAU has entered into a joint stewardship arrangement with the Hopi Tribe whereby ceremonial images may still be viewed onsite at the Cline Library; however, such images will not be shared on the Internet.[13]

RETHINKING TRADITIONAL ARCHIVAL PRACTICE

Caroline R. Arms, technical program coordinator for the National Digital Library at the Library of Congress, writes that "the importance of a collection may lie in its overall scope and relationships among its parts; preserving the archival integrity of a physical collection is a guiding principle for curators. Online systems for archival pictorial collections should allow the user to wander within the boundaries of a collection, with easy access to collection-level information that provides an intellectual context for the entire body of material."[14] Cline Library staff have struggled with the question of how best to achieve archival integrity while quickly connecting users with content, the "stuff" of history, across and within collections. Physical arrangement has no relevance in the virtual world. How much and what sort of description is necessary (i.e., original item-level data, collection-level data, digital object metadata)? What is the role of natural language? How will the work-flow change? How will geographically dispersed collections be reunited? The staff view planning for the new digital tool as an opportunity to rethink current practice.

Unlike a human-readable letter or photograph which remains intelligible after residing untouched in a box or a closet for a half century or more, a digital product–both the content and the media–must be refreshed, migrated, and/or reformatted throughout its life cycle to ensure access and usability. Much scholarly literature has been written about digital preservation and the colossal losses associated with inattention to documentation and maintenance. For instance, up to 20 percent of NASA's data from the 1976 Viking mission to Mars, collected by the Jet Propulsion Laboratory, has been lost. Quoted in *Newsweek*, Abby Smith of the Council on Library and Information Resources mused, "The more technologically advanced we get, the more fragile we become." Suffice to say, digital archaeology will be a growth profession.[15]

IMPLICATIONS FOR REFERENCE SERVICES

The Special Collections staff has experienced some interesting twists in providing virtual reference assistance in a real-time world. Diane Nester Kresh of the Collaborative Digital Reference Service (CDRS) affirms that "What Internet users need, they say, is human intervention to locate answers that are fast, personalized, easy to find, and free, at least for the time being." The department maintains fairly traditional hours with limited staffing. Although the typical response time to an e-mail or telephone query is 24 hours or less, the Cline Library is not yet in a position to offer live reference assistance around the clock. The CDRS international model for routing references requests may not be applicable to archives, due to the unique nature of the materials.[16]

Contextual ambiguity abounds in the digital environment. Is the person requesting assistance local or a thousand miles away? Yahoo, AOL, and Hotmail addresses offer no clue. Powerful search engines, such as

Google, generate misleading hits by drawing upon keywords in the digital exhibits or content tool. A favorite, *monthly* request goes something like this: "I am interested in purchasing a camel. What kind of camels do you have and what do you charge?" The confusion stems from a historic reference in the virtual exhibit "Flagstaff History For Kids!" to the introduction of camels to northern Arizona in the 1850s as experimental military pack animals. The military released the camels into the wild during the Civil War, and the last confirmed Arizona camel sighting occurred in 1911. The NAU archivist jokes about selling camels as a post-retirement career.

Some patrons assume that everything in the archives is digitized. "Why not?" inquires the disappointed researcher. Special Collections is in the midst of revamping the departmental Web site to better clarify which digital products and services are available. Many archives recognize the value of a "Frequently Asked Questions" section. Another expectation on the part of the digital patron is access to interactive order forms and electronic payment for high resolution scans or publication-quality reproductions of images, oral histories, films, and manuscripts. Electronic delivery is preferred, whenever possible. Even language barriers become more apparent with a global presence. Staff has exercised rusty skills in French, German, Italian, and Spanish to interpret e-mail.

CONCLUSION

Archival collections exist to be *used*; documentary materials have the power to change lives. A content-rich digital database greatly expands the possibilities for distributed learning, for instilling a deeper appreciation of the past, for understanding the present, and for imagining the future. In 1995, Michael Gorman challenged archivists and librarians "to serve humanity, to respect all forms by which knowledge is communicated, to use technology intelligently to enhance service, to protect free access to knowledge, and to honor the past and create the future."[17] By integrating new functions into current programs, the NAU Cline Library's digital offerings support Gorman's Five New Laws of Librarianship. Archivists intend to be part of the digital revolution, despite fiscal and technological obstacles, and to continue a long tradition of service to society, onsite and online.

NOTES

1. Susan Alden, "Digital Imaging on a Shoestring: A Primer for Librarians," *Information Technology and Libraries/Communications*, 15, no. 4 (December 1996): 247-250.

2. Meg Bellinger, "OCLC Digital and Preservation Resources: Delivering on the Technology Promise," *OCLC Newsletter* (September/October 2001): 23. For additional information about EAD and SGML standards, consult the Library of Congress EAD standards page <http://www.loc.gov/ead/> and the Society of American Archivists EAD Roundtable Help Page <http://jefferson.village.virginia.edu/ead/>. Accessed November 13, 2001.

3. The Digital Library of Georgia <http://mars.libs.uga.edu:80/index.html> and the Denver Public Library <http://gowest.coalliance.org> also deserve recognition for their contributions to development and dissemination of digital collections. Accessed November 13, 2001.

4. Bonnie Holmes, " 'Keeper of Treasures' Treasures Role," *Horizons* (1999): 36.

5. For information about the Dublin Core, consult <http://dublincore.org/documents/dces/>. Accessed November 15, 2001.

6. Special Collections and Archives experienced a 20 percent per year increase in onsite visitation and exponential growth in e-mail reference queries for the first few years of the database's operation.

7. "Other Digital Image Collections" <http://sunsite.berkeley.edu/Collections/otherimage.html> and "Internet Scout Project" <http://scout.cs.wisc.edu/index.html>. Accessed November 13, 2001.

8. The Institute of Museum and Library Services awarded a generous grant to Southern Utah University for "Voices of the Colorado Plateau" <http://archive.li.suu.edu/voices/voices.swf>. Accessed November 15, 2001.

9. Steven Puglia, "The Costs of Digital Imaging Projects," *RLG DigiNews*, 3, no. 5 (October 15, 1999) <http://www.rlg.org/preserv/diginews/diginews3-5.html#feature>. Accessed November 20, 2001.

10. Caroline R. Arms, "Getting the Picture: Observations from the Library of Congress on Providing Online Access to Pictorial Images," *Library Trends*, 48, no. 2 (Fall 1999): 379-409.

11. Elizabeth F. Farrell and Florence Olsen, "A New Front in the Sweatshop Wars?" *The Chronicle of Higher Education* (October 26, 2001): A35-A36.

12. An Arizona Revised Statute A.R.S. 39-121.03(D) stipulates that a state agency will assess a charge for commercial use which reflects the value of the item "on the market."

13. The Cline Library will not duplicate a ceremonial image without permission from the Hopi Cultural Preservation Office.

14. Arms, "Getting the Picture," 393. It should be noted that the Library of Congress also encourages cross-collection searching.

15. Arlyn Tobias Gajilan, "History: We're Losing It," *Newsweek* (July 12, 1999): 47. As a starting point for learning more about digital preservation, consult the 1996 report authored by the Task Force on Archiving of Digital Information entitled, "Preserving Digital Information," <http://www.rlg.org/ArchTF/tfadi.index.htm> or Caroline R. Arms, "Keeping Memory Alive: Practices for Preserving Digital Content at the Na-

tional Digital Library Program of the Library of Congress," *RLG DigiNews*, 4, no. 3 (June 15, 2000) <http://www.rlg.org/preserv/diginews/diginews4-3.html#feature1>. Accessed November 20, 2001.

16. Diane Nester Kresh, "Offering High Quality Reference Service on the Web," *D-Lib Magazine*, 6, no. 6 (June 2000) <http://www.dlib.org/dlib/june00/kresh/06kresh. html>. Accessed November 20, 2001. The September 2001 (v. 20, no. 3) issue of *Information Technology and Libraries* is devoted to Internet reference services.

17. Michael Gorman, "Five New Laws of Librarianship," *American Libraries*, 26, no. 8 (September 1995): 784.

Partnering to Build a State Portal: MyCalifornia

Kristine Ogilvie
John Jewell

SUMMARY. The Governor of California announced a completely re-designed, new state portal as part of his efforts to improve services to the public through a broad customer-centric eGovernment initiative. The California State Library was a core part of the subject content team and partnered with other agencies to develop in 120 days MyCalifornia <http://my.ca.gov>. This article explores: (1) the principles and objectives for the new portal; (2) the evolving role the California State Library had within this project; (3) the questions that a library should answer before undertaking such an effort; and (4) the benefits that such opportunities can bring. *[Article copies available for a fee from The Haworth Document Delivery Service: 1-800-HAWORTH. E-mail address: <getinfo@haworthpressinc.com> Website: <http://www.HaworthPress.com> © 2002 by The Haworth Press, Inc. All rights reserved.]*

KEYWORDS. California, state government, state portal, state Web sites, state library, eGovernment

Kristine Ogilvie (kogilvie@library.ca.gov) is Senior Librarian for the State Portal, Government Publications Section, California State Library, 914 Capitol Mall, Sacramento, CA 95814. John Jewell (jjewell@library.ca.gov) is Chief, State Library Services, California State Library, 900 N Street, Sacramento, CA 95814.

[Haworth co-indexing entry note]: "Partnering to Build a State Portal: MyCalifornia." Ogilvie, Kristine, and John Jewell. Co-published simultaneously in *Internet Reference Services Quarterly* (The Haworth Information Press, an imprint of The Haworth Press, Inc.) Vol. 7, No. 1/2, 2002, pp. 31-47; and: *Database-Driven Web Sites* (ed: Kristin Antelman) The Haworth Information Press, an imprint of The Haworth Press, Inc., 2002, pp. 31-47. Single or multiple copies of this article are available for a fee from The Haworth Document Delivery Service [1-800-HAWORTH, 9:00 a.m. - 5:00 p.m. (EST). E-mail address: getinfo@haworthpressinc.com].

INTRODUCTION

Most libraries are part of larger organizations, whether of state government like the California State Library, federal or local government, universities, or corporations. Few are independent entities. They support their parent institutions and their clientele. The focus, however, is upon the library's specific services rather than the overall role of the larger institution.

In his State of the State Address in January 2001, Governor Davis announced a completely redesigned, new state portal as part of his efforts to improve services to the public through a broad customer-centric eGovernment initiative. The California State Library had the fortune to be a core part of the subject content team for this Web site–MyCalifornia <http://my.ca.gov or http://www.ca.gov>.

MyCalifornia serves as the primary portal to California state government information. It provides an interactive means for the people of California–as well as others interested in the state from this country and the world–to find the information and services for their lives, business, work, and travel from the convenience of their offices, schools, and homes.

Usage is high. There are one million hits to this state portal each day. It is the guide to over a million pages of information in the widely-used ca.gov and state.ca.us domains. The ca.gov domain ranks fourth in the use of government Web sites, including the major federal home pages. There were 2.89 million *unique* users of California state Web sites in February 2001. It was the only non-federal Web site in the top ten most heavily used government sites in the country.[1]

The intense efforts by State Library staff to identify, organize, and develop good content in the initial phase of the portal–from the start of the project in September 2000 to its release 120 days later–brought recognition and reward. Arun Baheti, California's Director of eGovernment, said in an interview published by the *Center for Digital Government* that "the librarians did the 'heavy lifting' in developing how content would be presented on the site . . . [and that] the librarians had been so crucial to the early roll-out of the portal that their services have become integral to the future of e-government in the Golden State."[2] While MyCalifornia is still very much in development, it received the 2001 Best of the Web award for state government Web sites from the Center for Digital Government and *Government Technology* magazine in August.[3]

The State Library now has responsibility for the continued development and enhancement of the state portal's information architecture, content, and taxonomy. Its role will include revising and enhancing the broad topical guides; developing the portal's state agency-wide database of Frequently Asked Questions (FAQ); responding to suggestions from the public through the "Let the Digital Librarian guide you" feature; improving search engine relevancy through standard metadata tagging throughout state Web sites; and development of a government services taxonomy.

The State Library knows, however, that its role is only a part of the overall state portal. For the public, MyCalifornia is also the applications developed by other state agencies in the eGovernment initiative–for registering with the Department of Motor Vehicles, finding a campsite, or locating a certified nursing home. Underneath MyCalifornia lies a complex infrastructure of hardware and software within state data centers to support quick database-driven response, personalization, certified accessibility, and real-time notification to text cell phones and PDAs. It was a greater project than a library would undertake on its own, whether in scope, scale, number of staff, level of use, sophistication of information technology, or time frame. Becoming part of such a large undertaking means being willing to become part of a team. The library must submerge its separate identity and relinquish the overall control it would normally have. In this article, the authors hope to explore: (1) the principles and objectives for the new portal; (2) the evolving role the California State Library had within this project; (3) the questions that a library should answer before undertaking such an effort; and (4) the benefits that such opportunities can bring.

PRINCIPLES AND OBJECTIVES
FOR THE NEW STATE PORTAL

This complete redesign of the state home page originated through a new state administration focus on eGovernment resulting in a formal Executive Order issued by the Governor in September 2000.[4] The approach was to be based upon best practices for information technology management and business processes. A high-level Web council would be created that would be comprised of top Silicon Valley executives. A new Director of eGovernment would be appointed to coordinate eGovernment activities.

Key to the Executive Order was implementing "a statewide Internet portal that offers a single, convenient access point for state government information and services." People would have a common customer-centric entry point to state services organized around their needs, not government organization charts. The portal would be enterprise-wide across all state government offices, as well as the legislature and the courts.

Those charged with developing the portal quickly agreed upon basic design objectives for a new state Web site that would represent "California . . . the birthplace of the Information Age." The primary objective was ease of access. No information was to be more than three clicks away. Content would be dynamic, capable of being personalized. Accessible to all, the user interface would meet the requirements of the Americans with Disabilities Act. In addition, the portal would have a completely redesigned information architecture and improved navigation. A new search engine would improve the timeliness and relevancy of results. Users would know that they were on a state government Web site through a new consistent look and feel, a design not only on the portal, but also eventually on all agency pages.

Underneath, the portal was to have strong content management capabilities, so that staff who knew programs and services rather than technical staff could submit content. The content management software would include a workflow management process to allow appropriate review and approval. Versioning would support rolling back to earlier versions if needed.

The first phase, including the development of the portal, was to be completed four months hence, in time for the State of the State Address in January 2001. The pace would be fast track even by dot.com standards, let alone government standards. Given this tight time frame, work on the portal project was divided into teams. These ranged from subject content–the team including the State Library–to those focused on the underlying application software, hardware, security and communications.

EVOLVING ROLE OF THE STATE LIBRARY
IN MyCalifornia

While the State Library became part of the development of MyCalifornia early in the process, its role evolved as it became clear what the library could contribute. It began with a simple inquiry about criteria for the search engine. The response was another question, "Would the State Library assist the project?" Anyone who knows the State Librarian, Dr. Kevin Starr, knew that his answer would be a strong, positive, emphatic "yes." Its role would be to help with the subject content, however that would come to be defined.

The structure of the MyCalifornia Subject Content Team that was quickly formed suggests the role that the State Library would eventually have. The team consisted of: the Director of eGovernment; a representative from the Governor's Office of Communication; the Director for Executive Information Services (that oversees the information technology operations for the Governor's Office); a MyCalifornia project director to coordinate between the various teams; consultants from Deloitte Consulting and Roundarch; and the California State Library (CSL) State Portal Team.[5] Under this high-level oversight, the State Library would not merely help–it would be its staff who would actually develop the subject content.

Inventorying and Identifying Resources and Models

The first charge was to inventory the current and previous California home page to identify what might be useful. This process was not one simple review. CSL staff made three passes through the previous sites. The first relatively quick pass was to develop a feel for its contents and a sense of any problems (one librarian suggested that it was to develop a "module consciousness"). The second pass was a careful review within each category of all links to determine whether they were still current and appropriate for a new Web site. The final pass was to confirm the earlier work, explore other relevant state Web sites for additional links, and identify gaps in coverage or balance.

A related but separate step was reviewing the home pages of all other 49 states as well as any award-winning government Web sites. The focus was on useful models, information architecture, categories of information, or interesting features.

Determining People's Questions

Looking at what has been done is helpful, but it does not identify what people are looking for. The CSL State Portal Team asked that agency managers look at what the public needed throughout their organizations. The message to them was: "When you are looking for frequently asked questions . . . ask the people at the front desk, the telephone operators and the people who open the mail. I don't think there's anywhere else in an organization where people know more about what is being asked."[6]

In addition, the team surveyed librarians in California about their clients' questions about state government through questionnaires to Federal and state depository libraries and to the Infopeople project.[7]

Creating the Basic Structure

As Rosenfeld and Morville state in *Information Architecture for the World Wide Web*, "The foundation of almost all good information architecture is a well-designed hierarchy" and that, while big Web sites may have more than one structure, "the top-level, umbrella architecture for the site will almost certainly be hierarchical."[8] That means first identifying the major content areas. Services in state government range from issuing drivers' licenses to promoting tourism, from helping people find jobs to fighting forest fires. The Subject Content Team worked together to identify major customer-centric themes for the new portal.

A starting point for the top-level categories, or tier one, grew out of a subject-based 1998 version of the state home page that had been well received. Some of the categories appeared obvious because of their importance, such as Government, Business, and Education (which was expanded to be Education and Training to recognize the lifelong learning needed today). At one meeting, a member of the team suggested linking travel with environment until it was pointed out that it did not seem appropriate to provide a guide to toxic waste sites in a section that promoted tourism. While business includes aspects of employment, the team wanted workers to find the programs and services created to help them in its own top-level category, Labor and Employment.

The number of top-level categories was limited to nine: Education and Training, Health and Safety, Business, Consumer and Families, Labor and Employment, Travel and Transportation, History and Culture, Government, and Environment and Natural Resources.[9]

Even while the decision was being made on these top-level categories, CSL State Portal librarians had been working on logical groupings of services, programs, and information that would make up each of the nine modules. Creating the tier two and tier three sub-categories was not a straightforward process. Tier two and tier three were developed in a complementary fashion, often at the same time. As a second tier heading became apparent, possible third tier subheadings might be listed, if nothing more than to give an idea as to what would be included in that section of the module. Alternatively, several types of programs might be listed, later to be grouped into a broader tier two. The team decided that, ideally, the structure should have no more than three tiers. That was not always possible. There are a few fourth tier headings. Below are some of the tier two headings from the Business Module:

Business Facts and Figures
eCommerce and High Technology
Beginning a Business in California
Permits and Licenses
Helping Businesses Succeed
Workforce
Tax Information and Forms

In addition to the specific headings, each of the nine modules had four second-tier headings that were standard across all the modules: (1) Laws and Regulations; (2) Policy Sources; (3) Agencies; and (4) Frequently Asked Questions.

Developing Content

The subject modules serve only to lead to information about specific issues, programs, and services. That is the real content people are looking for. The challenging, yet fun, part was locating links to the appropriate government information to provide content and preparing good annotations. The CSL State Portal Team spent hours surfing agency Web sites as well as becoming well acquainted with the Google search engine, in particular its government information search feature, Uncle Sam, to find appropriate links to populate the nine subject modules. Like any good library collection, the resources had to meet certain standards, both of quality and of authorship. They had to be a government or government-sponsored Web site.[10] Members of the team met with policy specialists from the California Research Bureau and with staff from other agencies to help develop the content for each of the nine modules. In addition, they incorporated resources to address the questions supplied by the documents librarians and Infopeople staff into each of the modules.

The CSL State Portal Team proposed and the larger Subject Content Team agreed upon a format for the resources: name, URL, author attribution, description. The name of the link would indicate what the link was about, not necessarily what the agency called it on its own site. The author or authority for each link would be identified at the agency level both to provide credit to the agency that provided the information and to help educate the public about who was responsible for that topic. Finally, the description would provide sufficient information to indicate whether the site was likely to be useful. Phrases, synonyms, and other terms that might prove helpful to someone searching the portal were included. Below is an example from the section on "Bringing Your Business to California" in the Business module:

> Incentives for Investing in California–*California Technology, Trade and Commerce Agency*
>
>> Learn about incentives for investing in California including targeted tax incentives, employee training, financing assistance and others.

A second example is from the section "For Parents" in the Education module:

> Immunization–*California Department of Health Services*
>
>> Learn about school and child care immunization and vaccination requirements.

During the initial 120-day phase, the CSL Portal Team created a few thousand such entries, so that the state portal would have significant content.

Building the Frequently Asked Questions Database

The questions gathered from librarians, agencies, and e-mails provided a valuable resource for developing the structure and content. That process also supported the development of a complementary access tool, a database of Frequently Asked Questions called the "How Do I . . . ." guide. It suggests "Let the Digital Librarian guide you." The FAQ database is another way for people to find readily what they were looking for. For example, local and national newspaper articles often report on the shortage of qualified teachers in California. The FAQ databases provide:

> *Question:* "I hear that California needs teachers–where do I find more information?

Answer: "The CalTeach Web site, sponsored by the California State University Chancellor's Office, provides all the information you need to find out how to become a teacher in California.

California will need nearly 300,000 teachers in the next 10 years, especially in urban and rural areas, and in the fields of math, science, special education and bilingual education. Prospective teachers can learn about the requirements for becoming a teacher, how to find a job, and available events and resources that could help."

Related items:

"Becoming a teacher in California–California State University Chancellor's Office–CalTeach."

Several hundred of the most frequently asked questions of state agencies are now in this database.

Creating an Agency Index

Librarians appreciate simple indexes. CSL staff argued for creating an index to all agencies that would allow people to go quickly to a department whose name they knew. The initial reply had been that the search engine would eliminate the need for an agency index. Two months into the project it became clear that there was no metadata or standard indication within agency pages that would automatically lead to the home page of an agency or department. Could the CSL Portal Team create a tool? Yes, it could and did. The State Agency Index is consistently the most frequently used part of the state portal.

Improving Relevancy in the Search Engine

The search engine portal team, which had begun spidering all the state Web sites, discovered problems returning relevant results. Agency Web pages generally lacked metadata. The language in the pages was another problem; it was correct in terms of legislative intent or legal requirements, but frequently not public-friendly. Page after page lacked the phrases that many people would use to search. The solution for the initial 120-day implementation was to search first the subject modules the State Library had developed and the Governor's Web site. These search results were relevant and could be further limited by the user through the major subject categories.

Subsequently the State Library was asked to develop standards for metadata and metatags; then to work with Verity, Inc. on the curriculum for a series of workshops to help agencies improve their metadata. An additional step, now underway, is to develop a taxonomy that will enhance mining of the state's Web information.

WHY BECOME PART OF AN INSTITUTIONAL PORTAL?

When libraries are asked by their parent organizations to be involved in a portal project, they may be inclined to respond with an immediate "yes." Certainly, whenever the Governor's Office requests assistance from the State Library, the State Librarian of California is likely to say "yes," particularly for projects deemed important. There are, however, appropriate questions to ask before taking on a major role in a general or institutional portal.

Is the Portal Appropriate to the Mission/Goal of the Institution? Does It Significantly Enhance the Institution?

Despite the fall of many dot.coms, portal remains a popular buzzword. Portals can provide organizations with increased visibility, better customer service, and other benefits. Developing the right model and business plan remain the challenge.

There is no question in 2002 that a state government should have a state home page guiding people to information and services by, about, or from its agencies and departments. Each state has a presence on the Web. The challenge is to have one that significantly improves people's access to information and services.

Is the Portal Appropriate to the Mission/Goal of the Library?

Not all institutional portals fit well with the role of the library. A corporation Web site may focus on marketing. If the library is primarily focused upon research and development, then promoting sales, while important to the existence of the corporation, may not fit well within the scope of the library.

For the California State Library, improving public access to state government information is clearly part of its role. Its mission statement reads: "The State Library is California's public research library that helps a diverse people, their governments and their libraries meet their knowledge and information needs." Throughout much of its 150-year history, the State Library has provided access to federal, state, and local government information to the people of California. A specific unit, the Government Publications Section, has served as the major resource in California for public access to state government documents and reports since 1909.

Is the Library's Role in the Portal Within Its Core Competency?

Many libraries provide some level of Web services and a library home page. There is great variation in the range of their sophistication and depth. Libraries also differ significantly in the level of information technologies and expertise.

The California State Library is a medium-sized library, a relatively small state agency. Its information technology bureau is focused on the integrated library system and personal computer support. Its staff did not undertake developing software applications, overseeing telecommunications, ensuring security, or providing 24/7 server support for the portal.

For MyCalifornia, the primary role for the California State Library has been in understanding the information needs of the public and the subject content. These are valid, traditional roles and strengths for librarians. They use their reference skills to listen to people, understand their questions, discern the underlying needs, and find the information that would help. They use their cataloging skills to organize information, describe the resources, and create multiple points of access. They provide collection development–to develop selection criteria for what would be in the portal, and to identify and select good resources.

Are the Resources Available Within the Library to Support the Project Initially? To Support the Project Long Term? Will the Project Bring Additional Resources?

Ideas are essential. They are fun and exciting. Turning them into reality takes people, time, and hard work. If the portal is to continue, then ongoing commitments for staffing, technology and software, and other resources need to be understood.

Given the importance of MyCalifornia, Dr. Kevin Starr, the State Librarian, made support of the development of the portal a library-wide effort. That made the project possible in the initial phases. Redirection of limited staff within the Government Publications Section was appropriate given the charge. As responsibilities transitioned to an ongoing role, the state's eGovernment leaders have supported additional resources including staffing.

BENEFITS OF PARTICIPATING

The State Library staff and management benefited greatly by working with the Governor's Office of eGovernment in the development of the new state portal. The primary ways through which the library is affected by being a part of the state government-wide portal team are:

- Impacts to Service
- Depth of Human Resources
- Depth of Technical Resources
- Invisible Benefits
- Impacts on Library Management
- Benefits to the State

Impacts to Service

Portal team members increased their understanding and knowledge of state government because of their role in locating and organizing the content for the nine subject modules. By having a better understanding of state programs and services, library staff are able to provide answers that are more complete. In particular, if staff know of services and programs that are offered cross-agency, they are better able to locate the needed information more efficiently. For example, if a staff member receives a question about which state agencies offer assistance in obtaining appropriate business permits and licenses, he or she would be able to direct that person to the California Technology, Trade and Commerce Agency as well as the California Environmental Protection Agency, both of which offer business permit and licensing assistance. The agency's name alone does not always reveal what type of information can be found on its Web site. For example, information about sales tax is found through the California Board of Equalization.

As a result of participating, the library has added new services. Currently, members of the CSL State Portal Team assist state agencies in devising taxonomies and incorporating metatags into Web pages and other electronic resources to provide better access to state government information. The team works and consults with agencies to create and write Frequently Asked Questions (FAQ). Many of these questions will serve double duty as FAQs for the agency's page as well as being incorporated into the state portal's FAQ. Also, there are plans to offer workshops to state employees on locating state government information on the Internet.

To provide expanded or new services, it is necessary to train staff in new applications, methods, and processes. Several of the staff have attended an intensive week-long "boot camp" in using Microsoft Access® to create databases to help organize and track the different portal projects. While staff were primarily trained to work on the state portal, their new skills can and will be used for other projects relating to the library.

Although new services related to the portal are being added, some other projects and services offered by the library must be scaled down. Major programs and services, however, are not directly affected. Some services may be impacted indirectly, as other staff members must step in to take extra reference desk time or perform additional duties related to the operation of the library.

Depth of Human Resources

By collaborating with the State on the portal project, the library team has the opportunity to work with information technology and computer industry experts. These experts provide more than technical assistance in installing software or implementing applications. They provide an informational avenue to find out about new trends in IT and computer industries. Even more useful are best practices from other Web projects and creative techniques to improve the usability of the portal. The burden of having to be the expert on any given program is not as great for library staff as they can turn to experts to resolve a technology issue. Some outside consultants provide in-house staff training on their products, which the library may not have been able to afford without being a part of the government-wide team.

In addition, the library's involvement with the state portal allows staff to work with experts within state government. Throughout this project, the library has worked with state information technology staff as well as agency program staff to develop the information contained on the portal. This has proven to be a marvelous way in which to promote the skills of librarians as well as increase the visibility of the library in state government.

By teaming with state experts and outside consultants to create the portal, the library was able to offer and receive guidance in the development of the portal's information architecture, thereby allowing the library portal team to gather pertinent information, gain a better understanding of software and hardware, and work more effectively at problem solving to create a better product.

Depth of Technical Resources

The ability to use the best of breed hardware and software, which the library would not have been able to afford on its own, was of great benefit to the library. Some of the technology that is used to run and maintain the portal includes:

- *Interwoven*'s TeamSite, Open Deploy and Templating for content management, versioning and workflow;
- *BroadVision*'s One-to-One for dynamic presentation and personalization of content;
- *Verity*'s K2 Toolkit for high-powered search and content retrieval;
- *Kana*'s (formerly *Broadbase*) eCommerce for analytics and eCustomer relationship management.

Powering MyCalifornia are 16 high performance servers: 4 Sun 420R Servers for BroadVision; 2 Sun 420R Servers for Interwoven; 2 Sun 420R Servers for iPlanet; 2 Sun 420R Servers for Verity Search; 1 Sun 420R Server for Verity Spider; 2 Sun 420R Servers for Oracle; and 3 NT Servers for Kana.[11]

Participating provided the library's portal team with access to people who understand these products and their capabilities and, in implementing the portal, were willing to help library staff understand their strengths and limitations.

Invisible Benefits

Several benefits to the staff and to the library are not readily apparent. Working with the larger organization can motivate and refresh staff by creating a means to learn new skills and by providing an avenue for career development. The scale and scope of the project allowed the portal librarians to use their skills in reference, cataloging, and collection development in new and creative ways, which not only helped retain staff, but may also help in the recruitment of new librarians to the State

Library and into the profession. Others in state government have started to view librarians as information professionals–as knowledge managers and information architects–not just as keepers of books.

Participation in the state portal forced the State Library to assume a much more active leadership role as both a provider and organizer of information to those within state government and to state citizens. Others within state government began to recognize the value of the library, which has led to some new state portal projects. The State Library is currently teaming with two county governments and the state Department of General Services to develop a model county-level portal information architecture that may be used by other counties in California.

Bringing these skills from within the State Library to other agencies, bureaus, and departments has created a team that promotes a unified and customer-centric state government, which ultimately benefits the citizens of the state. It allows a citizen to find the information he or she needs without spending long hours trying to figure out which department's Web page may have the answer. For example, a California businessperson may need information on business taxes in the state. He or she can browse the Business subject module on the state portal or use the state portal search engine to locate the information quickly. Business taxes are regulated by three separate agencies. These agencies have created a combined Web site[12] where a businessperson can go to find information on sales tax, employment tax, and income tax without having to guess which agency will provide the information he or she needs.

Impacts on Library Management

As the library became a permanent member of the State Portal Team, library management had to reevaluate staffing levels, workload reallocation and position descriptions. At least one full-time staff member is now assigned as lead to coordinate and take responsibility for the library's role on the state portal team.

The library's budget will be affected by working with the larger organization. There are cost savings in equipment, software and staff. Nonetheless, there may be costs associated with the training of staff members, such as in database creation or use of other off-the-shelf type products. The travel expense line of the budget may have to be increased to cover conferences, speaking engagements, or consulting opportunities.

Benefits to the State

While the focus here is on benefits to the library, there have been benefits to the State. eGovernment leaders found knowledge, skills, and expertise in the State Library that would otherwise have had to be hired outside of state government, costing more and taking longer. There was no need to bring the consultants up-to-speed on the organization and politics of state government. The CSL librarians already understood the organization of state government, knew how to organize information in ways that are meaningful to the public, and were expert in identifying and finding the information people needed.

Overall, partnering on MyCalifornia has provided the State Library with a new way of providing service to the citizens of the state as well as to state officials and agencies. The library has become a major resource within state government for organizing information, for information architecture, and for content management.

NOTES

1. Shawn P. McCarthy, "Heavy Traffic Travels to Federal Web Sites; Government Activity," *Government Computer News* 20, no. 9 (April 20, 2001): 36.

2. Darby Patterson, "Lights May Dim but California's Portal Shines," Center for Digital Government. Filed: June 2001. Available: <http://www.centerdigitalgov.com/center/highlightstory.phtml?docid=2530000000002566.0>. Accessed: December 24, 2001.

3. Rhonda Wilson, "The Center and GT [Government Technology] Name the Best Government Web Sites," Center for Digital Government. Filed: August 2001. Available: <http://www.centerdigitalgov.com/center/highlightstory.phtml?docid=3030000000002714.0>. Accessed: December 24, 2001.

4. Governor Gray Davis, "Executive Order D-17-00," September 8, 2000. Executive Order D-17-00 may be found on the Governor's Web site at <http://www.governor.ca.gov>. Select the Press Room, then Executive Orders, and September 2000. Accessed: December 24, 2001.

5. The CSL State Portal Team had a core of six staff: John Cornelison, Senior Librarian for Internet Services with the California Research Bureau; Pat Zografos, Senior Librarian for Internet Services with Library Development Services; Lois Shumaker, catalog librarian from the California Research Bureau; Karen Smith, cataloger from the California History Room; and the two authors, Kris Ogilvie from Government Publications Section, and John Jewell, then Assistant Director for Information Services with the Research Bureau.

6. Darby Patterson, "Librarians Booked for Portal Project," *Government Technology's Electronic Government*, A Supplement to *Government Technology* (Summer 2001): 28-29.

7. Infopeople is a project created by the California State Library in late 1993 to assist public libraries to provide public access to the Internet, eventually placing over 500 Internet workstations in libraries around the state and training staff on their use. Its current primary role is to "provide broad-based technology-related training for those working in California libraries." Available: <http://www.infopeople.org>. Accessed: December 24, 2001.

8. Louis Rosenfeld and Peter Morville, *Information Architecture for the World Wide Web* (Sebastopol, CA: O'Reilly & Associates, 1998): 36-46.

9. George A. Miller, "The Magical Number Seven, Plus or Minus Two: Some Limits on Our Capacity for Processing Information," *Psychological Review* 63 (1956): 81-97. Available: <http://www.well.com/user/smalin/miller.html>. Accessed: December 24, 2001.

10. There are a few exceptions to this rule. For example, there is a link to Mapquest Maps and to Yahoo Maps in the Travel and Transportation module.

11. For additional general background and technical information on the portal, see a presentation by Mark Price, the primary consultant from Deloitte, "My California: Setting the Direction for e-Government." Available: <http://www.doit.ca.gov/cio_meeting/My_CA_4_04_01/index.htm>. Accessed: December 24, 2001.

12. "Tax Information Center: Your Business Taxes." Available: <http://www.taxes.ca.gov/index2.htm>. Accessed: December 24, 2001.

Moving Towards a User-Centered, Database-Driven Web Site at the UCSD Libraries

Laura Galván-Estrada

SUMMARY. In the summer of 1999, the libraries at the University of California, San Diego (UCSD) embarked on a Web redesign project. Essential to the new Web site were the development of a database of resources, Sage, and the creation of various in-house tools, which are used to enter and edit database resources. Tools were also created which assist in the creation and maintenance of various Web sites. With the completion of the project, UCSD students, faculty and staff can easily locate the resources and library information they need and library staff have more tools for Web site management. *[Article copies available for a fee from The Haworth Document Delivery Service: 1-800-HAWORTH. E-mail address: <getinfo@haworthpressinc.com> Website: <http://www.HaworthPress.com> © 2002 by The Haworth Press, Inc. All rights reserved.]*

KEYWORDS. Web site redesign, portal, Web site management, Web development, library Web sites

INTRODUCTION

Like most academic libraries, the University of California, San Diego (UCSD) had developed a large, complex Web site to provide ac-

Laura Galván-Estrada (lgalvane@ucsd.edu), is Web Services/Reference Librarian, Social Sciences and Humanities Library, University of California San Diego, La Jolla, CA 92093-0175.

[Haworth co-indexing entry note]: "Moving Towards a User-Centered, Database-Driven Web Site at the UCSD Libraries." Galván-Estrada, Laura. Co-published simultaneously in *Internet Reference Services Quarterly* (The Haworth Information Press, an imprint of The Haworth Press, Inc.) Vol. 7, No. 1/2, 2002, pp. 49-61; and: *Database-Driven Web Sites* (ed: Kristin Antelman) The Haworth Information Press, an imprint of The Haworth Press, Inc., 2002, pp. 49-61. Single or multiple copies of this article are available for a fee from The Haworth Document Delivery Service [1-800-HAWORTH, 9:00 a.m. - 5:00 p.m. (EST). E-mail address: getinfo@haworthpressinc.com].

49

cess to resources and services for its students, faculty, and staff. The UCSD Libraries are made up of several geographically dispersed libraries as well as a number of specialized collections, each served by their own Web site. By the summer of 1999, library staff were maintaining almost 14,000 html pages, hosted on at least six Web servers, and pointing to over 25,000 non-UCSD e-resources. There were also about 8,500 online resources fully cataloged in the OPAC, ROGER. These disparate Web sites provided no consistent navigation schema, did not present a uniform graphical identity, and did not effectively use Web technologies. Search capabilities were rudimentary when they existed, and searching across all library sites was not possible. In order to use the site effectively, users were expected to be familiar with the organizational layout of the UCSD Libraries.

From a practical standpoint there was duplication of effort in developing and maintaining the pages. For example, subject specialists were maintaining lists of resources and duplicating those resources across multiple pages. If a resource changed its URL, that change had to be manually entered across all the static pages, whenever it was caught. Some subject areas in support of academic programs were not being adequately covered. Other areas of concern included a lack of uniformity among the libraries in link checking and generation of Web site usage statistics. In light of the above, library administration and other staff agreed that it was time to change the ways of creating and maintaining the UCSD Libraries' Web sites, in order to improve the sites for users and to make maintenance and creation of Web pages easier for staff.

AUTONOMY AND COLLABORATION

In the spring of 1999 a library-wide Web site redesign project was launched, known as the Portal Project. The goals for the new UCSD Libraries' Web site were to:

- meet users' information needs;
- incorporate existing Web-based information delivery systems;
- incorporate current Web technologies;
- incorporate all existing UCSD Libraries' Web pages;
- incorporate the California Digital Library;
- develop tools to enable Libraries' staff to easily incorporate digital content;

- provide user access to core services from any point within the UCSD Libraries' Web site;
- incorporate best practices for human-computer interactions.

In order to achieve these goals, a core Steering Committee was formed with representatives from a wide variety of departments and units: instruction librarians, bibliographers, public services staff, cataloguers, and programmers. This Steering Committee became known as the Portal Team. Over the course of the project, several smaller working groups were created to focus on specific project areas such as database design, author tools development, graphic design, usability testing, design and content of library services pages, and technical issues.

DEFINING THE DATABASE

The Portal Team determined that a database approach would assist them in accomplishing some of the goals of the project: a more user-centered, as well as more manageable way of maintaining resources. The database would be key in providing a powerful mechanism for dynamically generating the browse and search capabilities of the Libraries' Web sites as well as creating customized Web pages. Static pages would still play a role, at least for services pages (such as hours, locations, staff contacts).

The team began by exploring approaches used at other comparable institutions. While this was extremely useful, no one had exactly what was needed for the goals of the project. The team also reviewed commercial software but, again, did not find a suitable product that would provide the functionality needed. Two in-house projects provided valuable experience. One of the UCSD Libraries had already embarked on a database-driven Web site; and the campus Web site, also created and maintained by the UCSD Libraries, was migrating to a database-driven environment. Since there was a lot of programming expertise in the library and the support to expand as needed for the project, the team decided to create its own tools in-house.

Central to this initiative was an underlying relational database of selected resources, known in its developmental stages as the value-added database (VAD). Subject specialists, bibliographers and other content providers would populate this VAD and drive the success of the new Libraries' Web site. The value in VAD comes from the identification and selection of library-wide resources by the Libraries' subject specialists and the addition of descriptive data elements to aid in the retrieval and display of these resources for the user. Just as subject specialists build the print collections, they are also responsible for building the electronic collections.

The database streamlines the creation and maintenance of Web pages by reducing redundant work for subject specialists/authors and facilitating the sharing of resource data among them. Authors can thus focus on the evaluation and selection of resources rather than on creating and maintaining html pages. Each record in the database describes one resource that will appear as part of one or more Web pages. Database records form the content for dynamically created Web pages that are assembled "on the fly."

Authors enter records for resources that are important for their subject area: principally online but, where appropriate, these may be CD-ROMs, printed books, etc. They assign one or more subjects, types/formats, and additional terms that enable the retrieval and display of customized pages. Other authors may add their own subjects or other data elements to resources, which already have a record in the database. These various data elements expand the opportunity to retrieve and display the resource in ways that meet a variety of user needs. Using the multiple page building tools, authors can use records from the database to generate pages with a great variety of formats. For example, a record for an article database, coded properly, can make that article database appear in a subject browse page, in a pathfinder created for a class, or in an alphabetical list of databases used in a specific library.

The resources in the database also "feed" a Netscape Compass search engine, which creates an academic version of a search engine that functions similar to Hotbot or AltaVista. Each record has a spidering depth level feature, and resources are added to this part of the database according to the spidering depth specified by the subject specialist. The search box provided for users allows them to perform the free-text searches they have come to expect with commercial search engines but in an academic context.

The public version of the VAD, browseable by subject or type and with the addition of the keyword searching, has become Sage.

ROGER and Sage serve different purposes. ROGER is the UCSD Libraries' database of record, the formal mechanism for bibliographic control of and access to the physical and virtual collections. Electronic resources continue to be cataloged in ROGER. Whole categories of electronic resources (currently, journals, newspapers and serial government documents) are managed by ROGER, and exported regularly from ROGER into the VAD. As more electronic resources are acquired, decisions are made on a case-by-case basis to determine if other categories of records should be exported from ROGER.

The technical foundation of Sage is a relational database, which was initially running in Sybase and has migrated to Oracle since the original launch. The browse functionality is provided by locally written Java servlets and Server-Side include Javascript applications that access the relational database. For more information about the Sage architecture, visit <http://libraries.ucsd.edu/about/sag-arch.html>.

SUBJECTS AND TYPES

The subject vocabulary used in the VAD, developed in close consultation with library subject specialists, reflects UCSD's academic and programmatic needs. It was originally attempted to use the subject terms used by the California Digital Library (CDL) Directory, a guide to electronic resources maintained on behalf of all libraries in the UC system. Some modifications were necessary, however, as the CDL vocabulary did not always meet UCSD's needs. Mindful of future collaborative efforts, subject terms from the CDL directory where shared whenever possible. The subject specialist for a given field is considered the owner of a subject but authors may use subjects not owned by them at their discretion, in consultation with the owner as necessary.

Below is the hierarchy of subject terms as of December 2001. *Arts* is expanded to its deepest level as an example:

> Physical Sciences and Engineering
> > Engineering and Technology
> > Physical Sciences
> Biology and Medicine
> > Biological Sciences
> > Medical Sciences
> Social Sciences and Humanities
> > Arts
> > > Architecture
> > > Art
> > > Dance

    Film Studies
    Music
    Photography
    Theater
  Ethnic Studies
  Gender and Women's Studies
  Language and Literature
  History and Area Studies
  Philosophy
  Religion
  Social Sciences

A list of types to qualify resources in each display in terms of format/genre was also developed. It was strongly felt that a user not only seeks information on a certain subject but also of a certain format. Types were much harder to define and some proved problematic. Users of Sage are able to browse all resources within any given type but they make the most sense within a subject display. The current list of types includes article databases, dissertations and electronic journals as well as more unusual types such as university sites, web megasites and even fun things (including entries for Baseball Almanac, L. A. Murals, Britney Spears' Guide to Semiconductor Physics)! Scope notes to assist authors in choosing the most appropriate type(s) were developed and an abbreviated version of these notes were made available from the public Web site. The Sage types as of December 2001 are listed in Appendix A.

Additional subjects and types are added and/or revised as subject specialists identify a need. There is an editorial board that reviews requests for vocabulary changes in types and subjects. For an example, due to the university's proximity to the border, the libraries receive a number of questions regarding U. S.-Mexico border studies. Even though UCSD does not offer a degree in this area, the Latin American Studies specialist felt it necessary to include United States-Mexico Border Studies to the subject terminology. Furthermore, a keyword feature to the record structure was added because the broad subject terminology may not go to the level of granularity needed for many resources. Authors can enhance their records by adding keywords to improve retrieval when searching Sage.

Also, to make specialized pages possible, a custom field feature was added. Authors can mark a record with as many custom field attributes and values as needed. For example, the alphabetical lists of databases needed by individual libraries as well as the well-known Reference Shelf are generated using custom fields.

As mentioned earlier, subjects are owned by a single bibliographer but as many authors as necessary share records. Authors are free to enhance existing records by adding subjects, types, keywords and custom fields as needed. Though restrictions could have been technically enforced, Sage authors chose to work in a culture of mutual trust. Authors negotiate changes in record descriptions as needed, rather than preventing anyone but the owner of a subject from editing records. These social controls have worked and a stricter access control system has not been necessary.

POPULATING THE DATABASE

A set of *author tools* was created to assist Sage authors in entering, editing and retrieving records. The set of tools grew over the course of the project and currently include not only tools for authors but every tool available related to Sage, such as web statistics, tools for creating public pages, and link checking. A full collection of documentation for the tools is also available through the *author tools*.

To take advantage of the many existing subject static pages, a tool called the *link grabber* was developed. With the *link grabber*, the author supplies the URL of the Web page containing the links, the number of links s/he wants it to grab, and which subjects and types should be globally assigned to those URLs (see Figure 1). Brief VAD records are created and the author can then go back to each record and enhance it. Through the use of an additional tool, the *record selector*, authors can retrieve and edit records based on any criteria.

The *new resource/edit resource* tools allow authors to add and edit resources. These forms include all the fields available in the database and are the most used tools to manually input new records (see Figure 2).

Another major tool is a synchronization procedure devised to automatically export records for electronic serials (including government documents and newspapers) from ROGER. The 690 field is used with the heading "electronic journals" followed by the appropriate VAD subject heading(s) and this tag is used in the export procedure. Each

FIGURE 1

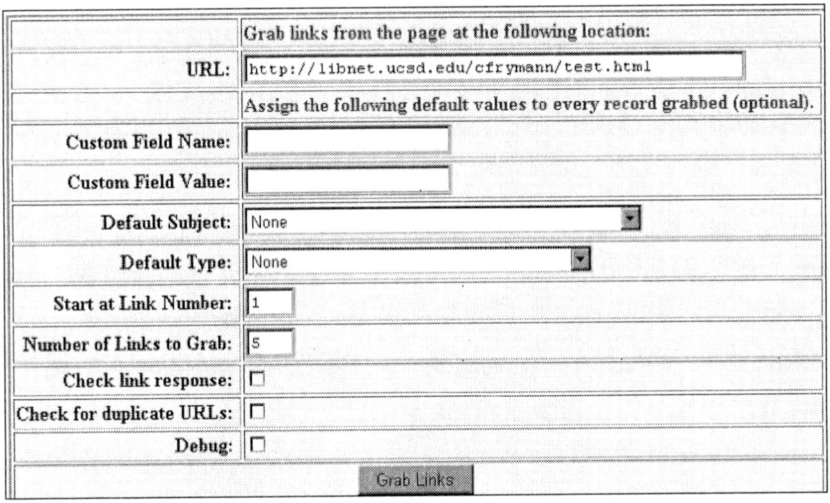

	Grab links from the page at the following location:	
URL:	http://libnet.ucsd.edu/cfrymann/test.html	
	Assign the following default values to every record grabbed (optional).	
Custom Field Name:		
Custom Field Value:		
Default Subject:	None	
Default Type:	None	
Start at Link Number:	1	
Number of Links to Grab:	5	
Check link response:	☐	
Check for duplicate URLs:	☐	
Debug:	☐	
	Grab Links	

electronic journal record is retrieved from ROGER in XML format, converted to SQL and inserted into the database. To account for electronic journals that are received as parts of packages but do not necessarily fit into UCSD's programmatic needs, and to be able to grab them through the synchronization procedure, some subject headings exist only for electronic journals, such as *paranormal*. Once these records for electronic journals are in the database, they can be enhanced, with the exception of the title, long description and URL.

HOW SAGE CURRENTLY WORKS

Sage is featured on the Libraries' Web sites as the "Gateway to Recommended Resources." The major public features of Sage are:

Browsing by Subject or Type

The browse screens provide access to records in the VAD. For a resource to appear in a Sage browse screen, its VAD record must contain at least one subject and at least one type. Records can be browsed by subject, hierarchically or alphabetically, and by type within a subject.

FIGURE 2

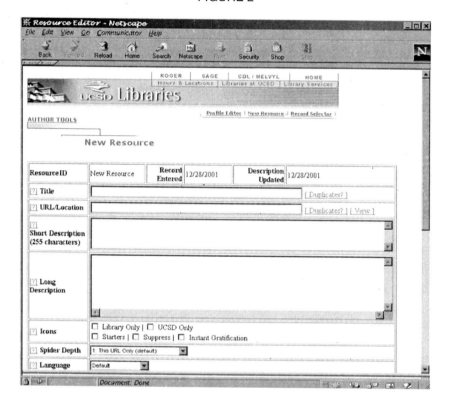

The initial screen of a subject browse displays featured items for that subject. For any subject added to a record, the author can specify whether the resource is major or minor within the subject, and can tag them as featured to display first. The list of types for any resource sort alphabetically in a table of contents on the right of the display, with the number of resources next to each type (see Figure 3).

Some changes in terminology were made at the beginning to achieve the desired displays. For example, it was decided that the type *article databases* would always display at the top. Accordingly, the current type *university sites* was changed from its original *academic sites*.

Browsing Electronic Journals

Electronic journals are the only type of records that can also be browsed within subjects in their own hierarchy, as this was a crucial

FIGURE 3

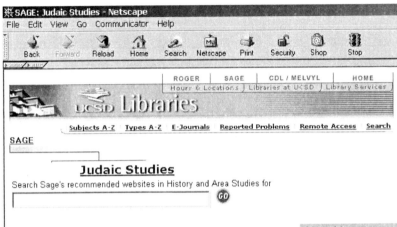

SAGE: Judaic Studies - Netscape

File   Edit   View   Go   Communicator   Help

Back   Forward   Reload   Home   Search   Netscape   Print   Security   Shop   Stop

ROGER   SAGE   CDL / MELVYL   HOME
Hours & Locations   Libraries at UCSD   Library Services

UCSD Libraries

Subjects A-Z   Types A-Z   E-Journals   Reported Problems   Remote Access   Search

SAGE

Judaic Studies

Search Sage's recommended websites in History and Area Studies for

[GO]

Article Databases

1. **ATLA Religion Database** KEY SITE [UCSD Only]
1949-present. Indexes journal articles, books and collected essays on all
aspects of religious studies. [Full Description]
URL too long to display
Journals indexed

2. **Index to Jewish Periodicals (CD-ROM)** KEY SITE [Library
Only]
1988-present. On SSHL Reference CDROM network. Comprehensive,
annually published guide to articles, book reviews, feature stories, and other
contents in English, appearing in more than 140 periodicals devoted to
Jewish affairs. [Full Description]
book://YCD162 | SSH Reference CDROM
Earlier years, 1963-1996, available in print

3. **Old Testament Abstracts (CD-ROM)** KEY SITE [Library Only]
1978-present. Available on SSHL Reference CDROM Network. Abstracts,
all written in English, cover works from many different languages including
journal articles, monographs, multi-author works, and festschriften.
[Full Description]
book://YCD33 | SSH Reference CD-ROM

4. **RAMBI: Index of Articles on Jewish Studies** KEY SITE
1966-present. Selective bibliography of articles in the various Jewish studies
and in the study of Israel. Material listed in Rambi is compiled from
thousands of periodicals and from collections of articles - in Hebrew,
Yiddish, and European languages. [Full Description]
http://libnet1.ac.il/~libnet/rmb/rmb.htm

5. **America: History and Life** [UCSD Only]
1964-present. International database for research on all periods of U.S. and
Canadian history. Includes abstracts of journal articles and listings of books

This Subject By Type:

Article Databases(18)
Bibliographies(1)
Biography(3)
Book Databases(13)
Book Reviews(1)
Conferences and Proceedings(2)
Directories(2)
Discussion Groups(2)
Dissertations(3)
Electronic Journals(37)
Electronic Journals (Collections)(3)
Electronic Texts (Collections)(3)
Encyclopedias(1)
Expeditions and Historical Sites(1)
Finding Aids to Manuscripts and Archives(2)
Fun Things(1)
Libraries, Archives and Historical Societies(2)
Literary Criticism(1)
Museums and Galleries(1)
News(19)
Pictures/Images(5)
Primary Sources(2)

need, especially for the science libraries. As mentioned earlier, the subject vocabulary for browsing electronic journals expands to account for electronic journals acquired in large packages that may fall outside of the primary subject areas.

Searching

When a user performs a search in the Sage search box, results are retrieved from a Netscape Compass database built from four types of material:

1. Recommended Resources:
   VAD resources that were selected and evaluated by subject specialists. The search terms are picked up from title, description and keywords in records.
2. Library pages:
   A selection of library Web servers spidered for html static pages. The title of the page and metadata assist in the retrieval of these results.
3. Electronic Journals:
   Electronic journals imported from the ROGER Catalogue that match the search criteria.
4. Additional Web pages:
   Records automatically entered in the database as a result of the spidering depth marked in the VAD records. Electronic journals are excluded from the spidering process. The resources in this part of the results have not been evaluated by a Sage author but have been spidered from pages that were selected by UCSD libraries' subject specialists.

FUTURE DEVELOPMENTS

As mentioned at the beginning of the article, a more uniform graphical identity and a consistent navigation schema were also part of our project. These goals have been accomplished for a vast majority of library Web sites but compliance with the formatting guidelines has proven harder than expected. The team continues to work with Webmasters on this issue.

Even though the database can handle any type of records, it is mainly composed of electronic journals, databases and Web sites. The inclusion of more diverse types of materials, such as digital audio and electronic reserves programs, for which other systems are used, is a high priority. In addition, the team would also like to make more use of the custom fields to generate pathfinders and specialized pages. Lastly, it has been suggested that users would like the ability to personalize and customize the Libraries' Web Site. To evaluate if this is indeed needed and provide that feature, the team would like to conduct usability studies.

CONCLUSION

As of November 2001, there were 15,626 records in the database: 10,461 of those were electronic journals; 170 subjects and 58 types were represented; and 107 custom fields and 6,760 keywords were being used. Even though some static pages are still being maintained, there are far less than before. Link checking has improved and there are now capabilities for generating web usage and Sage statistics. Searching within and across the different Libraries' sites is now possible. The Web sites of the UCSD Libraries have accomplished a consistent navigation schema and common graphical while being able to share records for generating pages and enabling branch libraries to meet the specific needs of their constituencies.

Sage can be found at <http://libraries.ucsd.edu/sage/> and additional information about the project can be found at <http://libraries.ucsd.edu/sage/about/>.

APPENDIX A. Sage Types

Article Databases	Jobs
Audio	Libraries, Archives and Historical Societies
Bibliographies	Literary Criticism
Biography	Maps/Atlases
Book Databases	Market Research
Book Reviews	Museums and Galleries
Companies	News
Conferences and Proceedings	Patents
Data Sets	Performing Arts Reviews
Data Visualization	Pictures/Images
Dictionaries	Preprints and Working Papers
Directories	Primary Sources
Discussion Groups	Product Catalogs
Dissertations	Publishers
Electronic Journals	Regulations/Laws
Electronic Journals (Collections)	Research Guides, Pathfinders and Tutorials
Electronic Texts	San Diego Area
Electronic Texts (Collections)	Societies/Associations
Encyclopedias	Software
Expeditions and Historical Sites	Standards/Specifications
Finding Aids to Manuscripts and Archives	Style Manuals
Fun Things	Teaching Aids
Government Resources	Technical Reports
Government Resources, California	Tests, Measurements, Questionnaires
Government Resources, International	UCSD Sites
Government Resources, San Diego	University Sites
Government Resources, United States	Video
Grants and Scholarships	Web Megasite

HealthLinks:
A ColdFusion Web Application

Brian Westra

SUMMARY. Libraries are beginning to use Web applications as they grapple with sites of increasing complexity, and the move of more user services to the Web. This article reviews the basic concepts of a Web application, and outlines some of the features of the HealthLinks Web application and site <http://healthlinks.washington.edu> at the University of Washington Health Science Libraries, and the transition from a Java-based application to ColdFusion. *[Article copies available for a fee from The Haworth Document Delivery Service: 1-800-HAWORTH. E-mail address: <getinfo@haworthpressinc.com> Website: <http://www.HaworthPress. com> © 2002 by The Haworth Press, Inc. All rights reserved.]*

KEYWORDS. Web application, ColdFusion, database-driven Web site

WEB APPLICATION OVERVIEW

As much of the business world has embraced the Internet, e-commerce innovations and changing user expectations have prompted li-

Brian Westra (brian.westra@metrokc.gov) is Head Librarian, Hazardous Waste Management Program, 130 Nickerson Street, Suite 100, Seattle, WA 98109.

The author would like to acknowledge the following members of the HealthLinks team: Debra Ketchell, Deputy Director, Health Sciences Libraries; Leilani St. Anna, Information Management Librarian; Emily Hull, Head of Information Systems; Adam Garrett, Senior Computer Specialist; Casey Hagan, Student Programmer (ColdFusion database maintenance tools); Cliff Olmsted, Student Systems Administrator (Linux and Apache); and Joanne West, Usability Studies and Webtrends Reports.

[Haworth co-indexing entry note]: "HealthLinks: A ColdFusion Web Application." Westra, Brian. Co-published simultaneously in *Internet Reference Services Quarterly* (The Haworth Information Press, an imprint of The Haworth Press, Inc.) Vol. 7, No. 1/2, 2002, pp. 63-88; and: *Database-Driven Web Sites* (ed: Kristin Antelman) The Haworth Information Press, an imprint of The Haworth Press, Inc., 2002, pp. 63-88. Single or multiple copies of this article are available for a fee from The Haworth Document Delivery Service [1-800-HAWORTH, 9:00 a.m. - 5:00 p.m. (EST). E-mail address: getinfo@haworthpressinc.com].

braries to examine their own online services. In this process, librarians and systems staff are confronted with budgetary and staff constraints, the real or anticipated expectations of users regarding Web-enabled services, and a reluctance to embrace and internalize business and development practices and philosophy. However, libraries are clearly about customer service and any organization interested in improving customer service quality can benefit from examining the successful use of design and technology by excellent service companies.[1] It is therefore worthwhile to note library-oriented articles on portals,[2,3,4] database-driven sites,[5,6] and the confluence of electronic commerce and digital libraries.[7]

In this regard, middleware and Web applications are beginning to see judicious use by some libraries. An exact definition of middleware is difficult to come by, but in a general sense it enables interaction between components (database, e-mail, Web server), and simplifies the programming model for the developer.[8] Web applications are one class of middleware. Web applications can range from "static Web pages, to searchable site/dynamic Web pages, and applications that integrate with operational databases," including customer-driven Web transactions.[9] In a general sense, a Web application is

> a Web system (Web server, network, HTTP, browser) in which user input (navigation and data input) affects the state of the business. This definition attempts to establish that a Web application is a software system with a business state, and that its front end is in large part delivered via a Web system.[10]

These descriptions exemplify the influence that business practices and applications have had upon the terminology. In an excellent review, Fraternelli regards the Web application as "characterized by a direct business-to-customer relationship."[11] On a more concrete level, the technology should attempt to meet some or all of the following requirements:

- handling both structured and non-structured data;
- support exploratory access through navigational interfaces;
- high level of graphical quality;
- customization and possibly dynamic adaptation of content structure, navigation primitives, and presentation styles;
- support of proactive behavior (recommendation and filtering).[12]

Fraternelli points out that these requirements may be in conflict with the following technical and administrative objectives:

- security, scalability, and availability;
- interoperability with legacy systems and data;
- ease of evolution and maintenance.[13]

Web application servers will gain greater acceptance by systems staff as they prove capable of minimizing complexity in dealing with multiple platforms and standards, security, and system-level management functions.[14] Fortunately, a number of products are able to support these needs.

Most models of a Web application are based on a three-layer approach: presentation layer (user-friendly interface), business-logic layer (implements the logic and provides services to the presentation layer), and the system layer, which is responsible for data storage and network requirements.[15] Business logic can also be defined as the piece that "links activities, actors, and resources together within and between companies in buyer-seller relationships."[16] It is relatively easy to extrapolate this definition to the relationship between the library and the patron, e.g., someone using the online circulation systems to renew a book, or setting up a table of contents alerting service for their commonly read journals.

Falk provided some earlier concepts of database-enabled library Web sites or site components that were precursors or have been incorporated into Web applications, such as dynamic page generation, periodical lists, and full-text collections not found in the catalog.[17] These exemplify how Web applications can be used to improve online services to users. Antelman gives an excellent review of the concepts behind library database-driven sites, and the Web management opportunities afforded by Web application servers. Web applications may be a necessary step in building sites of increasing complexity, integrating heterogeneous, distributed resources, while affording some aspects of information management and organization to both library staff and the end user.[18] Application servers such as Macromedia's ColdFusion (tm) provide Web site integration tools, open database connectivity (ODBC) features, and integrated development environments (IDEs)[19,20] that allow developers to more easily construct Web applications.

HealthLinks OVERVIEW

The HealthLinks site <http://healthlinks.washington.edu/> is a critical resource for information for faculty, staff and students in the Health Sciences at the University of Washington. The site also serves the various medical centers associated with the university, faculty and students in the five-state WWAMI region (Washington, Wyoming, Alaska, Montana, and Idaho), and the public. Ketchell and Hull have provided a good overview of the site's history, and its utility as a portal for serving the medical clinician.[21,22] The site provides access to textbooks, journals, databases, and other relevant resources for students and faculty, as well as information for the clinician and researcher. Information is presented in the form of role-based "toolkits" (see Figure 1), and topical pages. Each toolkit is developed with and revised in response to user feedback. The site receives significant usage; a three-month average for autumn 2001 indicates the site receives approximately 16,400 hits per day, or 500,000 per month. Work on the site and the underlying database is a collaborative effort, and includes departmental liaisons, serials and systems staff, and others.

Like most library sites, HealthLinks was strictly "hand-maintained" HTML at its inception in 1994, and remained so until 1998. Under funding by an Integrated Advanced Information Management System (IAIMS) grant from the National Libraries of Medicine, a database was developed to maintain several thousand links to commercial and locally developed content. Apache Web server was and continues to be used for static HTML pages and CGI scripts. The move to the use of database content in 1998 was driven by several factors. These included a desire to reduce the number of hand-maintained HTML pages; to facilitate subject experts' access directly to the data and its organization that could be extrapolated to the site, rather than via HTML editing; and to improve search granularity that could not be achieved through a full-site search engine, but might be offered by a database approach.[23]

At the time of the move from flat text to a database-driven site, approximately 150 out of several thousand Web pages of the site were set up to be generated from a database. These 150 pages changed regularly to remain up-to-date and to reflect changing user needs, and were therefore optimal candidates for dynamic or database-generated content. The Java-based Web application wrote out the 150 pages to the Web server, and provided an interface through which library staff could enter and edit records and relationships in the database, which directly affected the organization and content of the generated pages on the site. Distrib-

FIGURE 1. The Student Care Provider Toolkit. This is one of the pages that is generated on a daily basis from the database. The topic is "Student Care Provider Toolkit," the categories are "MEDLINE and Full-Text Journals," "Drug Reference," "Key Resources," "Evidence-Based Medicine and Guidelines," etc. Resources are listed under each of the categories.

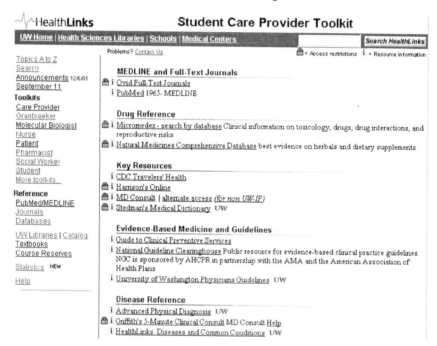

uted access to the database maintenance tools was important, since a variety of library staff do data entry and may work from home as well as the office. While this type of Web application is perhaps not as dynamic or synchronous as a shopping cart application for an e-commerce site, it provides a foundation for understanding the site in relation to current terminology. It is worth noting that library staff are also users of the site, as they use the public site and the database maintenance tools to provide instruction and information services and maintain electronic collections and serial subscription information.

The initial Web application was built with JavaServer page utilities and Java servlets to generate the Web pages and provide an interface for the data tools. Page generation was provided by combining information from database queries with HTML tags into text files that were then written out to the Web server. The database tools allowed staff to edit records and establish relationships in the database, which were used for these page generation queries.

The application utilized IBM Websphere application server[24] and a SQL Server 6.5 database with approximately 5,000 resource records. For the purposes of the HealthLinks database, a "resource" is a unique record, typically pointing to a Web site or specific online source, with information stored in a mixture of Dublin Core metadata and locally produced fields, including URL, title, and associated keywords (see Figure 2).[25] These resources can be grouped together within categories (and subcategories), which are then associated with one or more topics. The basic page of the site that is generated from the database has as its foundation a topic, and from zero to several categories with their respective resources. For instance, in Figure 1, the topic is "Student Care Provider Toolkit," and the categories are "MEDLINE and Full-Text Journals," "Drug Reference," "Key Resources," etc. The resources are the links under each category.

A Java programmer/project administrator and student programmers developed the database and Web application for the site, and it went through iterative changes during the next two years. While the site was successful by many metrics, the Java-based Web application required a programmer to make any changes in the database maintenance compo-

FIGURE 2. Table of Dublin Core metadata and locally produced fields associated with the Resource records.

Dublin Core Fields	UW Local Fields
Title	Topic
Resource Identifier	Category
Subject/Keywords	Subcategory
Format	Access Restriction
Language	UW Resource
Author	Class Number
Rights Management	Bookplate
Description	Help
Publisher	Notes
Other Contributor	Unique ID
Date Published	Record-Created-Date
Resource Type	Record-Last-Modified-Date
Source	Record-Created-By
Relation	
Coverage	

nents or the code that generated the HTML pages. In addition, some of the search capabilities that were an original goal of the transition remained unrealized, though Java could have been used for this feature.

CONVERSION PROJECT

In 2000 it was decided to convert the entire Web application from Java to ColdFusion for the next iteration of the HealthLinks site. This decision was based on several factors, including: the flexibility afforded by the rapid development environment of ColdFusion; relatively low ongoing development cost compared to hiring a Java programmer; more intuitive approach to the code for non-technical staff; utility with both Windows and Linux platforms; and adoption of ColdFusion for Web applications by several other health sciences libraries.

The conversion from Java to ColdFusion focused on three components: (1) static page generation; (2) database maintenance tools; and (3) new dynamic pages and search features as they became possible. Several constraints were placed on this conversion phase. The database schema could not be altered, since the Java-based database maintenance tools would continue to be used while the site generation tools were being replaced by ColdFusion templates. Secondly, while the public site could not be substantially changed in its overall design, changes to improve workflow in the database maintenance tools and new search features for the public site were expected. The new Web application enabled the HealthLinks team to contemplate other components and search features for the site as the project progressed. At recent count, the number of generated pages had risen to 294, and there were 3,667 hand-maintained HTML files in the production site.

It is good practice to approach a Web application project from the perspective of a development cycle, even if the project itself will be based on rapid development and prototyping. The development cycle emphasizes requirement-gathering, modeling, and prototyping,[26] and is intended to help the development team clarify and meet checkpoints throughout the process, and avoid project "creep." Requirements throughout the project were based on the same site generation capabilities, database access, and workflows that were provided by the Java application. Once the database schema and queries had been established, a "proof of concept" group of templates were developed that could generate the same pages as the existing application. Following this the remaining page generation templates were developed and implemented. The final steps involved building new data entry tools, and this process was more iterative in nature since workflow improvements could be realized along the way with input by staff and librarians.

ColdFusion

ColdFusion Web application server is produced by Macromedia,[27] and when coupled with the Studio editor, provides a rapid development environment in which coding and scripting, database connectivity and queries, and HTML tags can be quickly combined within a single editor that is easy to personalize and reconfigure (see Figure 3). ColdFusion allows the developer to address issues related to multiple platforms and standards, security, and system management on several levels, in the

FIGURE 3. ColdFusion Studio editor provides an integrated development environment for editing CFML, HTML, and accessing the database tables to quickly build queries.

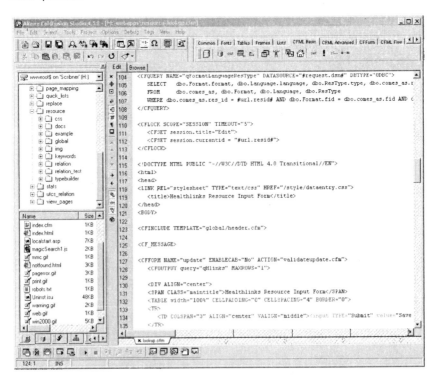

code that constructs the application, and through configurations in the server administration console.

ColdFusion employs a tag-based approach to programming, where functionality is encompassed within tags rather than needing to be explicitly scripted, and offers some familiarity to those acquainted with HTML, as its namesake ColdFusion Markup Language (CFML) implies. Some understanding of relational databases and structured query language (SQL), and an affinity for basic programming concepts will be useful for those new to application development. Advantages of the use of ColdFusion are the ease and speed of application development due to the tag-based coding features,[28] cross-platform capabilities, a large user base and support forum. Libraries use ColdFusion for various applications.[29-39] Developers are not limited to the present group of CFML tags, since user-defined functions and custom tags can be created for specific purposes, and there is a library of custom tags on the Macromedia site. It is generally easier and faster to create functional applications using ColdFusion than by the use of more complex Web application platforms, such as Active Server Pages (ASP)[40] and PHP, though there are plenty of library applications built with those tools.[41] Ultimately, the choice of an application server is highly dependent on considerations that should include staff skills, training, financial resources, preexisting software and hardware, and a commitment from administration and systems to support the choice.

The basic setup for a ColdFusion application calls for a Web server (UNIX/Linux or Windows OS), with ColdFusion, and an ODBC database on the same machine or another.[42] A typical dynamic page generation occurs in the following way. When the Web server receives a page request that calls for a CFML template or other processing (.cfm or .cfml), it routes the request to the ColdFusion application server. The ColdFusion files ("templates") are written in CFML, and reside on the ColdFusion/Web server. When they are executed they may run queries against the database or do other processing, then combine this information with HTML tagging, and output the resulting file(s) to the client via the Web server.

Documentation

Many Web site developers fail to provide formal documentation, due to the iterative, user-centered approach that is taken with smaller and medium-size sites.[43] This can be true of any development process, and unfortunately, the database and Java-based tools lacked much of the information that would have eased the conversion. Therefore, another explicitly stated goal of the project was to develop clear documentation. The resulting ColdFusion templates contain numerous CFML comments about specific sections of code, and there are separate documents to provide overviews of the file generation templates, the database, database maintenance tools, and hardware and software configurations.

Database

Because the database and Java code lacked documentation, anecdotal information from the HealthLinks team and examination of the Java code were used to determine how the database schema evolved, and what role the various tables played. Several tables were found to be residuals from older revisions of the database design, and establishing their true role proved to be time consuming. This led to an incremental process for the development of the initial page generation templates, until all relevant tables and relationships were defined.

The current database schema is shown in Figure 4. The most basic content component of the HealthLinks database is the resource record. The database diagram shows how resources are related to keywords and other descriptors of the resource. Resources are then related to specific Topic, Topic/Category, or Topic/Category/Subcategory groups, through the Include and Related tables. Further, most pages are generated from the database at the Topic level; that is, most of the pages have a single topic and zero to many categories.

A number of stored procedures are used in the Web application. Stored procedures allow a query to be optimized and stored on the database, rather than in the CFML. This enables the CFML code to be somewhat independent of the database schema, and in databases of larger size and complexity, stored procedures may provide some advantages in overall processing speed for the Web application. As part of the overall project, naming conventions were agreed upon for the stored procedures, and other components within the CFML such as query and variable names.

Site Architecture/Hardware

The ColdFusion Web application was developed in a separate environment from the live site and production database. A copy of the database was exported to a server running Windows NT (later Windows 2000), ColdFusion Web application server and Studio, Apache Web

FIGURE 4. HealthLinks database schema.

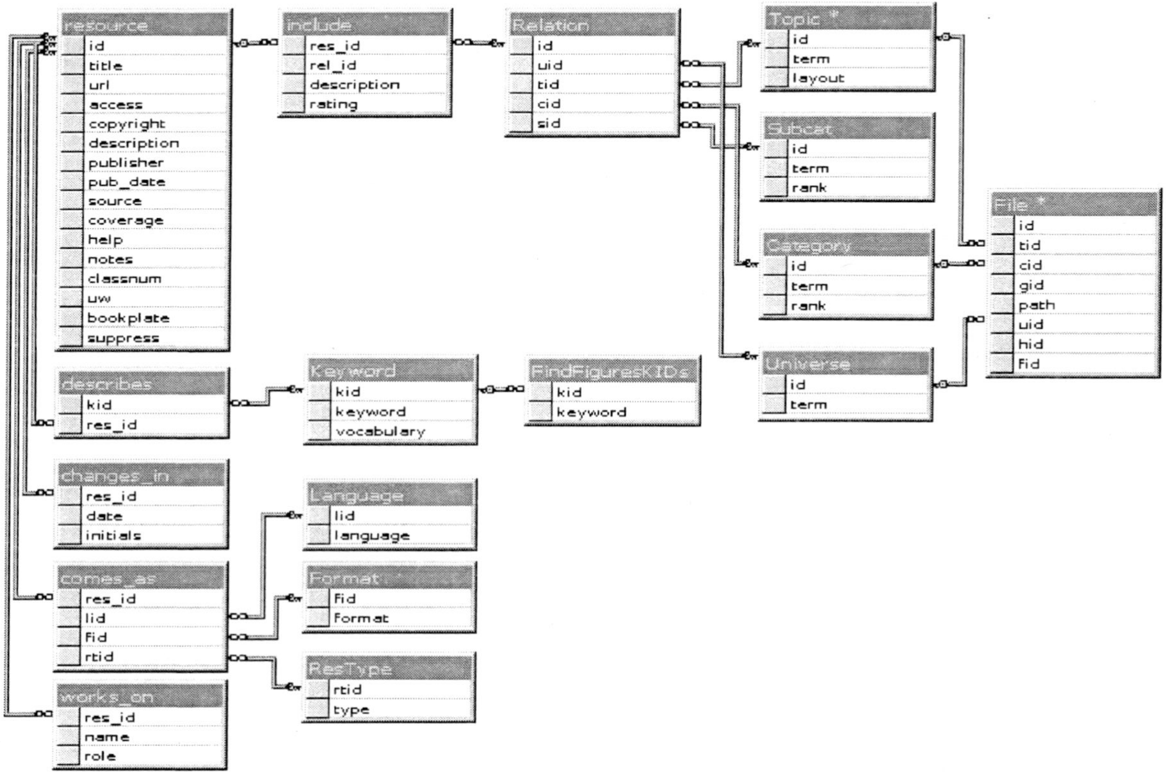

server (later Microsoft Internet Information Services 5.0), and Microsoft SQL Server 7.0. In time, a full development architecture was set up to mirror the anticipated production site. In an ideal world, production and development architectures would generally mirror each other, for purposes of working through configuration and site architecture issues, and load testing of templates before moving to the production server. In reality, suitable results for smaller sites with simple database back-ends can often be achieved with single servers for development and production. Some libraries have used file-based databases such as Microsoft Access, but larger and more complex databases and heavy Web loads usually require a client-server database, and segregation of the database server from the ColdFusion/Web server can improve performance.

Several older servers which were to be phased out were "recycled" into use for the development site, which was ultimately composed of an Apache Web server running on Linux, and two Windows 2000 servers, one running Internet Information Services (IIS) 5.0 and ColdFusion 4.5, the other devoted to SQL Server 7.0. The production site, which came online in April 2001, has four Dell 2,450 servers, with dual 733 MgHz processors, 1 Gb RAM, and 256 Kb cache. As with most dynamic sites, the greater the RAM, the better the capacity to cache pages and query results, and therefore to handle higher traffic loads. Two servers run Red Hat 7.1 and Apache, with failover between them, for the static HTML and CGI scripts of the HealthLinks site (see Figure 5). Another server runs Windows 2000 and is devoted to ColdFusion/IIS, where the Web application server and Web server run. The database (SQL Server 7.0) resides on the fourth server, also on Windows 2000.

The templates reside on the ColdFusion/IIS production and development servers. Several of the templates call stored procedures on the database, or directly query the database tables, and write out static HTML pages to the Linux/Apache machines. Other templates query the database and populate Verity indexes (called collections) for use with the Verity 97 search engine that comes bundled with ColdFusion. These collections provide full text, Boolean searches, and are run via ColdFusion templates as well.

Page Generation, Verity Indexing, and Logs

Basic queries of the database were tested to determine the correct relationships and optimal SQL statements, and these were later incorporated into the database as stored procedures. By combining the "order

FIGURE 5. HealthLinks production site architecture.

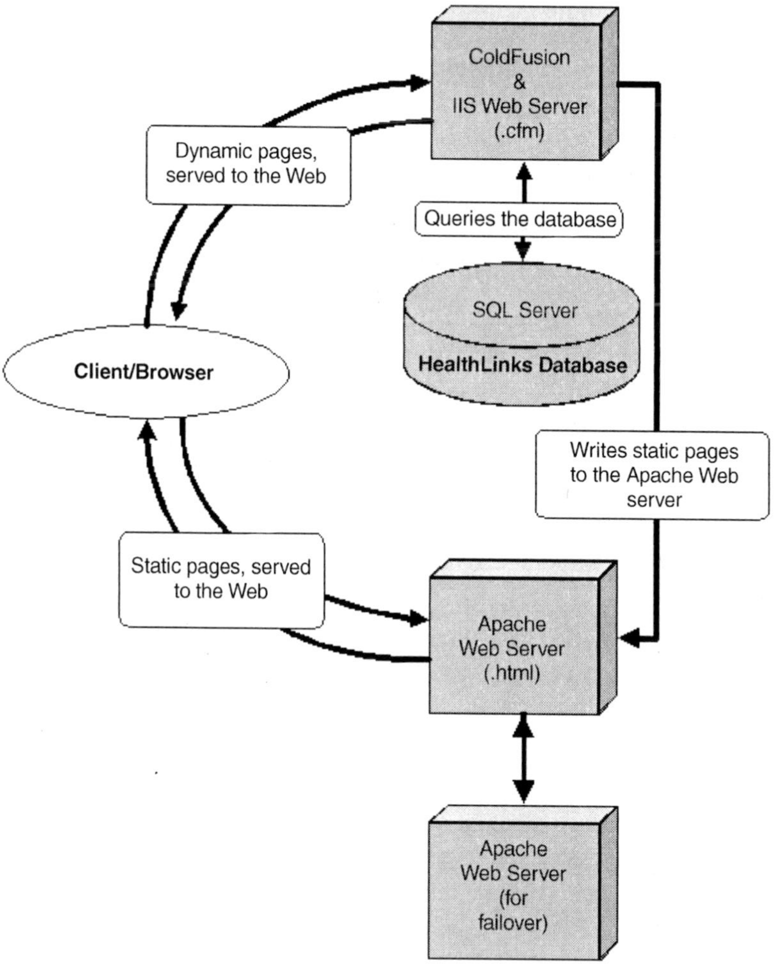

by" statements in the queries and nested output, various configurations of the resulting pages can be achieved.

Four templates have been created to write out static HTML files to the Apache Web server and ColdFusion server for the public HealthLinks site. These templates cover four types of pages, each of which utilizes a different query of the database. The templates generate topic/category pages, e-journal pages for browsing by journal title, topic/category/subcategory pages (Molecular Biologist toolkit), and statistics resources pages for browsing by topic. These pages may change from day to day, but the information is generally not so fluid as to require "on-the-fly" dynamic generation. In addition, the production and use of these static pages provide information that is up-to-date for the user, while reducing the overall load on the application server and database that dynamic pages would require.

HealthLinks makes use of server side includes (SSIs) to produce the navigational structures on the top, bottom, and side of each page. Apache can be enabled to include SSIs, but a Web server can only employ one type of server side processing on a given page. Since ColdFusion is a type of server side processing, ColdFusion templates can not use the SSI method, but instead use the CFML equivalent, called a <cfinclude> tag, which can point to a file with the .ssi, .cfm, or other extension. This allows the same SSIs to be copied across both Web servers for equivalent content and function in the static and dynamic pages, no matter what the server. In a limited number of cases, certain SSIs for the static and dynamic pages are generated on a daily basis, where the content of the SSI might change from day to day. For instance, the e-journal search box has an alphabetical title browse list, which may change as subscriptions are added or dropped, so this SSI is generated from the database, and written out to both the Apache Web server (for static e-journal pages) and the ColdFusion server (for e-journal title search results pages).

The ColdFusion templates call the stored procedures as specified in their code and use the results to write out HTML files to the appropriate directories on the Apache Web server. The page generation templates are scheduled to run once each day, overwriting the previous day's files. When these scheduled templates run, they also append information to a log file to record template name, query results, and which HTML files were generated.

Search Features

The HealthLinks site is popular, and the use of the Verity search engine that comes bundled with ColdFusion Web Application server has proven to be a scalable approach to searches that meets user needs. In the Java-based Web application, the only search option on the site was a full-site Web search, via a Webinator/Thunderstone search engine. Search results could have been configured to a greater degree, but users found the search results display confusing, and expressed a desire to have a more targeted search that would yield only the resources from the HealthLinks database, rather than whole Web pages.

Web site searches are now carried out via an Inktomi/Ultraseek search engine, which is run by the University Libraries. ColdFusion templates and the Verity 97 search engine provide the other search options on the site.[44] Any search request that originates on the HealthLinks site, including an Inktomi search, has its search terms recorded by a ColdFusion template before being processed. Hit counts are also recorded for all the Verity searches. This data will enable us to analyze the types of searches (journals vs. other resources), phrase vs. single term searches, and the relationship between search requests and navigational structures and terminology.

The primary search feature is the site-wide resources search, which searches titles and descriptions of resources in the HealthLinks database. The search form is located at the top of all HealthLinks pages, replacing the Webinator search, and therefore has become the default choice. The precise location of the search form and associated text was determined based on a small usability test. There were approximately 18,000 searches per month from September through October 2001; 12,000 were resource searches, 670 were Web site searches, and 5,000 were e-journal title searches.

The e-journal search is a new feature that accompanied the move to ColdFusion. It is accomplished via a Verity collection created by a query of the resource titles related to the e-journal topic. When a search is run against this collection, a list of resource ID numbers for matching e-journal titles is returned to the template. The ColdFusion template then runs a query of the HealthLinks database to return the related information for each resource ID. This information is put into alphabetical order, which is served to the client in an HTML file via the IIS Web server.

The resource search is also conducted against a Verity collection. This collection or index is built from a query that returns the titles and keywords from all "unsuppressed" resource records. Resources can be added to the database, but blocked from inclusion in Verity collections or site generation by means of a checkbox on the Resource data entry form in the database maintenance tools.

Another recently added search is an index of approximately 250 resource records for print and online statistical sources. This search employs a collection of titles, descriptions, and keywords created from a query of only those resources that contain the statistics keyword, which is used to indicate that a resource is primarily statistical in nature. This keyword is used to create this Verity index, and to generate approximately 130 static pages for browsing by statistical topic.

Load Testing

Load testing is a valuable tool,[45] but many libraries and smaller enterprises do not account for this in their development cycle. A primitive form of load testing was carried out by means of a ColdFusion template that could cycle at a specified time interval. The template ran a basic query of the database that employed relationships between several tables, and therefore provided a good approximation of a typical query. Multiple instances of the template were run, and parameters of the IIS server were logged for analysis. This testing indicated that the application as designed was scalable beyond the anticipated number of hits per minute.

Scheduling Template Activity

Templates for site generation and Verity collection indexing were scheduled to run daily, by means of the ColdFusion Administrator console. These templates and the database maintenance tools are run in a virtual directory with a different port number to isolate them from the search templates for scheduling purposes, and to allow their activity to be logged in a different IIS log than the search template activity. Because the templates are resource-intensive, they were scheduled to run at a time when public use of the site was lowest. However, it was later found that search engine spiders or robots indexing the site would hit all of the information links on a given page within the space of several seconds. Each of those links runs a query and dynamically generates a page. If this occurred at the same time as the CPU-intensive site generation templates were scheduled to run, the Web application server could slow down or lock up. Rescheduling the site generation templates countered this problem. Another possible solution is to generate static pages for all of the information links, rather than pulling them from a dynamic query, or to move more of the information for that part of the site to a database view, which would require less of the database server's resources. Timeout for the templates in the Scheduler is independent of the server-wide timeout setting (which was set to 10 seconds), and some of the scheduled templates take up to 25 seconds to run.

Database Maintenance Tools

Browser Compatibility. Because some of the templates in the database maintenance tools make use of JavaScript, it was decided to design this part of the Web application to use Internet Explorer (IE) 5.x, so that template development did not have to follow parallel paths to accommodate differences in how JavaScript is handled by Netscape and IE. This choice is possible since there is a limited population of librarians and staff working with the database tools, and they have ready access to IE on their desktop machines. Since IE was chosen, it was also decided to employ Cascading Style Sheets (CSS) for much of the display features, as CSS enables the developer to quickly and easily alter fonts, colors, and other Web page attributes, and IE does a good job of displaying standards-conformant CSS.

Pubcookie/UWNetID Authentication. Distributed secure access was enabled via secure sockets layer (SSL) with a Thawte certificate, and the PubCookie/University of Washington network ID (UWNetID) authentication system. Pubcookie is a centralized authentication system developed by the University of Washington Computing & Communications Department. It is composed of software installed on the server, and the Weblogin server administered by the University.[46] This software is available for Apache and IIS servers. The two components together enable a server administrator to authenticate user access to a particular Web directory by their UWNetID and password, and to set a timeout for this authentication. Upon authentication, a cookie is set. A ColdFusion custom tag was developed which tests the cookie value against a list of authorized UWNetIDs for that particular Web directory. Authorized users are allowed to use the application, while unauthorized users are bounced out to a different directory with an appropriate message. This method is simple, and while it has its limitations, it is adequate to the needs at this time.

Every time a user accesses a file in the database maintenance tools, Pubcookie checks for authentication via the cookie that is saved on the user's machine after the initial login. If the user is authenticated, the next step is that the custom tag is called from within that directory's Application.cfm template. The tag has several attributes that are passed to it in the call, including a list of allowed UWNetIDs, which are compared against the Pubcookie cookie value, and a message to users that are not in the list of authorized users.

Tools Overview. The database maintenance tools are a collection of ColdFusion templates aiding staff and librarians in the entry and organization of data in a SQL server database. The database maintenance tools integrate some of the following features: improvements in resource lookup; data validation rules; context-sensitive user authorization; user timeout; and automatic recording of the user doing record maintenance.

Components of the data entry tools are the ColdFusion templates, SQL Server database, and the Pubcookie software. As with the page generation templates, stored procedures on the database are used throughout this part of the application for increased performance and to isolate some of the database design/schema from the ColdFusion code. Another feature of ColdFusion, transaction blocks, is used for all activities that modify data in the database, whereby a series of queries is either enacted or completely rolled back if it is not completed. This protects data integrity across related tables. Custom tags and server side includes are employed to modularize the code and facilitate code reuse.

The database maintenance tools are not publicly accessible, but several screenshots and descriptions may illustrate some of the more pertinent features. Authorized users can modify resource records, topics, categories, subcategories, relationships between the parts of this hierarchy, and the name and location of the HTML file to be created for a particular topic. The user can also view lists of some of these records, such as the keywords and "orphan" resources that are not currently related to a particular topic but may be important to include for the public site's resource search.

A problem with the Java application became evident as the tables were reviewed. Several tables contained duplicate records, indicating that the business logic had not included sufficient data validation rules for all tables. These were incorporated into the new application, so that duplicates could not be entered. If a term that the staff person is attempting to add to the database already exists, the user is informed that it already is in the database. Otherwise, the term is added to the database, and the user is informed once the update is completed.

Editing Resources. The lookup template is the heart of the resource data entry templates, and was revised with input from staff to improve the workflow over the previous search and input forms. All fields are labeled, and required fields have red labels. The only restriction other than a required field is that the URL must be a unique value among resource records in the database. After clicking on the Save button, the fields are parsed and saved into the appropriate tables in the database. The template also checks to see if the resource record in the database has changed since it was delivered for editing.

If the validation process finds that the data has indeed been changed, it redirects the user to a page that displays the original information, along site information submitted by the user. In addition, for those fields where another user has revised the data, that information is shown. If the user wants to go ahead with the update, the template parses the new information again but the check for changed data is not initiated, and anything submitted over-writes the existing record in the database.

Relations Tree. One of the more complex display features is the relations tree form. The CFTree tag was used for the relations tree form, because it replicated what was found in the Java Web application, and its Java applet provided the necessary display and data manipulation functions (see Figure 6). In the right window is a CFTree containing all relations in the database that are available to be associated with the resource record being edited. The CFTree applet shows topics (folders), which can be expanded to show existing category components and their subcategories, if they exist. On the left are the current relations associated with the resource, again showing Topic, Category, and Subcategory. When a relationship is added or deleted, the windows update immediately, so the user can see which topics, etc., the resource is related to.

FIGURE 6. Relations Tree form, showing the relation options, and those that have been chosen for resource number 2222, Gene Tests. In this case, the resource has been associated with the Key Resources category, in the Pediatrics topic, among others (see the window on the left).

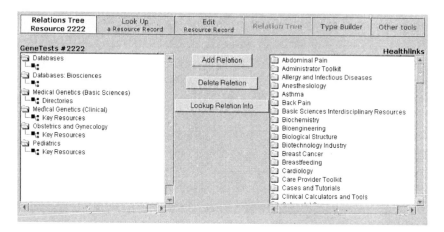

Universe, Topic, Category, Subcategory, and Relationship Tools. Individual universes, topics, categories, and subcategories can be added, deleted, or revised by means of a single group of templates. The universe table and relationships are a carryover from a previous version of the database. HealthLinks is currently the only universe, but this level in the hierarchy may be used at a later time. Code reuse for this group of data tools is made possible by custom tags that call for different functions, based on the information that is passed into them. For instance, working with topics passes the relevant table and query information into a common template that builds a form for either universe, topic, category, or subcategory data entry. Figure 7 shows the topic data entry form, but the same template builds the forms for editing universe, category, and subcategory records.

Whether the user is adding, deleting, or revising a record, a confirmation message is presented as part of the process, and in cases where the record is related to others, the user is given an opportunity to accept or decline the action before it takes place.

Relationships, Page Mapping, and Viewing Generated Pages. Several other forms complete the database maintenance tools. After the Topic, Category, and Subcategory terms have been entered into the database, they can be related to each other as a hierarchy (see Figure 8). Once these relationships are established, they will appear in the Relation Tree for the resources, and staff can then relate a selected resource to the particular Topic/Category (and Subcategory) combination.

Pages to be generated are given a specific file name and path in the Page Mapping tool, so they can be written to the Web server (see Figure 9). This information is stored in the File table in the database. Any of the pages to be generated can be previewed within the database tools so that staff can view it before it is generated as part of the production site.

CONCLUSIONS

The conversion to ColdFusion Web application server was successful, and has enabled the HealthLinks team to develop features on the site that had previously been long-term goals. Through their participation, non-developer team members also achieved a better understanding of the database schema, limitations and capabilities of a Web application, and the new opportunities that might be realized in a rapid development environment.

FIGURE 7. The form for editing/revising Topics in the HealthLinks database.

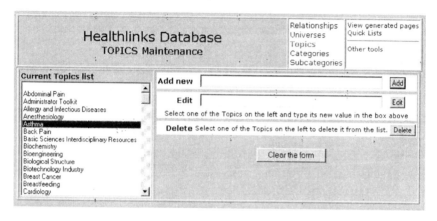

FIGURE 8. Relations tool, showing the relationships that exist (bottom window), and the options that can be selected to create a new hierarchy between universe, topic, category (optional), and subcategory (optional, but requires a category).

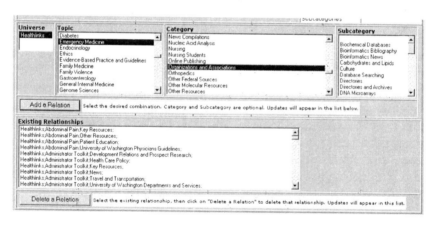

Documentation for any technical project is an issue that must be addressed in an ongoing manner. Lack of information can cause critical delays, particularly in environments where the institutional memory is crippled by staff turnover, and this proved to be the case with the transition from the previous HealthLinks Web application. Commenting out code and writing documentation are tasks that most developers would

FIGURE 9. Page mapping tool, to define the path and file name to which a generated page will be written on a daily basis.

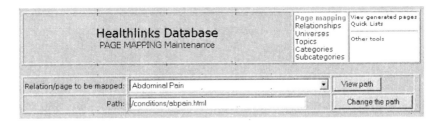

rather avoid, as they are time consuming and there is little immediate impact on the development process to show for it. It can also be difficult for an overworked manager to put together a rigorous review of the documentation in preparation for the worst-case scenario. However, project managers should give this component due emphasis throughout the development cycle.

A rapid development environment, such as afforded by ColdFusion, is valuable to the organization if the developer or team can avoid being caught up in a continuous prototype-test-prototype-test cycle. Clear requirements and checkpoints aided in this regard, as did a commitment by project managers to stay on task. An issue for some libraries may be the initial purchase cost for proprietary solutions such as ColdFusion. It is also important to remember the costs of development and long-term maintenance for any given approach, including the time to production, training, and staff and infrastructure requirements.

As has been noted, the resource search in the HealthLinks database became a reality with the new Web application, and it is extremely popular. Approximately 12,000 searches per month in the autumn of 2001 were resource searches. The revised but prominent placement of the search form on all HealthLinks pages, and emphasis on the utility of this new search feature in library instruction, will account to some degree for its popularity. The usability testing associated with the resource and Web searches showed that users are still confused about the differences between these two searches. Only about 670 searches per month were Web site searches, and this option is not as visible as the resource search. It is difficult to find terminology and a search interface that will clearly differentiate these two types of searches, and most users will simply change search syntax or terms, rather than investigate help files or search suggestions.

Other searches recently added to the site include the e-journal title search and statistics resources search. E-journal title searches accounted for another 5,000 searches per month. Logging of search terms and type of search will enable the HealthLinks team to more quickly analyze search strategies and their relationship to terminology, navigation structures, and organizational features. Dynamic page generation also allows staff to include links to URLs with embedded queries for inclusion of "on-the-fly" dynamic content, which previously was not possible.

Custom tags and server side includes are employed to modularize the code to some degree, though more could be done in this area, particularly if a Fusebox coding methodology was followed for the entire application.[47] This approach enables abstraction of the code and code reuse, and may enable future staff to quickly ascertain the functions of each template. However, this approach tends to take longer at the outset, and requires a higher level of programming in the development stage.

Future projects for HealthLinks may include improvements in the indexing terminology, and a refined resource keyword list would lead to improvements in searching.[48] Changes to the database schema may be considered at a later time, as will overall site design modifications. These issues are being investigated by means of other grant-funded projects, which can provide flexible, "test-bed" approaches to the use of the HealthLinks database for applications focused on more specific needs of clinicians.[49,50]

NOTES

1. Jane Kingman-Brundage, "Technology, Design and Service Quality," *International Journal of Service Industry Management* 2, no. 3 (1991): 47-59.

2. Debra S. Ketchell, "Too Many Channels: Making Sense Out of Portals and Personalization," *Information Technology and Libraries* 19, no. 4 (2000): 175-179.

3. Amos Lakos and Chris Gray, "Personalized Library Portals as an Organizational Culture Change Agent," *Information Technology and Libraries* 19, no. 4 (1999): 169-74.

4. Mick O'Leary, "Grading the Library Portals," *Online* 24, no. 6 (Nov/Dec 2000): 38-44.

5. Kristin Antelman, "Getting Out of the HTML Business: The Database-Driven Web Site Solution," *Information Technology and Libraries* 18, no. 4 (December 1999): 176-181.

6. Bryan H. Davidson, "Database Driven, Dynamic Content Delivery: Providing and Managing Access to Online Resources Using Microsoft Access and Active Server Pages," *OCLC Systems and Services* 17, no. 1 (2001): 34-42.

7. Nabil Adam, Yelena Yesha, Baruch Awerbuch et al., "Strategic Directions in Electronic Commerce and Digital Libraries: Towards a Digital Agora," *ACM Computing Surveys* 28, no. 4 (December 1996): 818-835.

8. Daniel M. Yellin, "Stuck in the Middle: Challenges and Trends in Optimizing Middleware," *ACM SIGPLAN Notices* 36, no. 8 (2001, August): 175-180.

9. Janet Butler, "Internet Applications: No Longer Toys," *Managing System Development* 19, no. 2 (February 1999): 1-9.

10. Jim Conallen, "Modeling Web Application Architectures with UML," *Communications of the ACM* 42 (October 1999): 63-70.

11. Piero Fraternelli, "Tools and Approaches for Developing Data-Intensive Web Applications: A Survey," *ACM Computing Surveys* 31, no. 3 (September 1999): 227-263.

12. Fraternelli, 228.

13. Ibid, 228.

14. Butler, 1.

15. Ezra Ebner, Weiguang Shao, and Wei-Tek Tsai, "The Five-Module Framework for Internet Application Development," *ACM Computing Surveys* 32, no. 1es (March 2000): Article 40, 1-7.

16. Seppo Leminem, "Business Logic in Buyer-Seller Relationships," *Management Decision* 39, no. 8 (2001): 660-665.

17. Howard Falk, "Library Databases on the Web," *The Electronic Library* 14, no. 6: 559-561.

18. Antelman, 176-181.

19. Richard Hoffman, "In the Middle: Enterprise-ready Web App Servers," *Network Computing* 10, no. 11 (May 31, 1999), Available: <http://www.networkcomputing.com/1011/1011r1.html>. Accessed: March 22, 2000.

20. Mark Cyzyk, "ColdFusion Markup Language," *Web Techniques* 5, no. 8 (2000), 3, Available: <http://www.webtechniques.com/archives/2000/08/junk/>. Accessed: December 8, 2001.

21. Debra S. Ketchell, Emily Hull, Leilani St. Anna, Wei-Laung Hu, and Leo Lai, "HealthLinks: Databasing a Web Site," Available: <http://healthlinks.washington.edu/primeanswers/cdl/8icml/>. Accessed: December 17, 2001.

22. Emily Hull, Leilani St. Anna, Kevin Ibrahim, Debra Ketchell, Micah Skilling, Constance Worley, and Steve Rauch, "HealthLinks: Databasing a Web Site," Available: <http://healthlinks.washington.edu/about/history/database/>. Accessed: December 17, 2001.

23. Ibid.

24. IBM, "IBM Software: Web Application Servers: Websphere Application Server: Overview," Available: <http://www-4.ibm.com/software/webservers/appserv/>. Accessed: January 2, 2002.

25. Hull.

26. Ming-te Lu and Wing-lok Yeung, "A Framework for Effective Commercial Web Application Development," *Internet Research: Electronic Networking Applications and Policy* 8, no. 2 (1998): 166-173.

27. Macromedia, "ColdFusion," Available: <http://www.macromedia.com/software/coldfusion/>. Accessed: December 15, 2001.

28. Mark Cyzyk, "ColdFusion Markup Language," *Web Techniques* 5, no. 8 (2000), 3, Available: <http://www.webtechniques.com/archives/2000/08/junk/>. Accessed: December 8, 2001.

29. E.A.B. Draffan and Robbie Corbett, "Implementing a Web-accessible Database," *The Electronic Library* 19, no. 5 (2001): 342-348.

30. Daniel L. Shouse, Nick Crimi, and Janice Steed Lewis, "Managing Journals: One Library's Experience," *Library Hi Tech* 19, no. 2 (2001): 150-154.

31. Ronald C. Jantz, "Providing Access to Unique Information Sources: A Reusable Platform for Publishing Bibliographic Databases on the Web," *Library Hi Tech* 18, no. 1 (2000): 28-36.

32. Arizona Health Sciences Libraries, Ejournals, Available: <http://www.ahsl.arizona.edu/journals/ejrnls/>. Accessed: December 17, 2001; Topics, Available <http://www.ahsl.arizona.edu/guides/topics/>. Accessed: December 17, 2001; Database and Digital Collections Listing, Available <http://www.ahsl.arizona.edu/guides/topics/>. Accessed: December 17, 2001.

33. Ben Forta, Forta.com, "Who's Using ColdFusion?" Available <http://www.forta.com/cf/using/list.cfm?categ_id=4>. Accessed: December 17, 2001.

34. Hofstra University, Available <http://www.hofstra.edu/home/index.html>. Accessed: December 17, 2001.

35. Lamar Soutter Library, University of Massachusetts Medical School, Ejournals, Available: <http://library.umassmed.edu/ejournals.cfm>. Accessed: December 17, 2001.

36. University of Texas Southwestern Medical Center at Dallas Library, Ejournals, Available: <http://www2.utsouthwestern.edu/cfdocs/library/ejournals/ejnls.cfm>. Accessed: December 17, 2001.

37. University of Wisconsin-Madison Health Sciences Libraries, Available: <http://www.hsl.wisc.edu/>. Accessed: December 17, 2001.

38. Virginia Commonwealth University, Course Reserves, Available: <http://www.library.vcu.edu/cfapps/ereserve/index.cfm>. Accessed: December 17, 2001.

39. J.W. Felts, "Now You Can Get There from Here: Creating an Interactive Web Application for Accessing Full-Text Journal Articles from any Location," *Library Collections Acquisitions and Technical Services* 25, no. 3 (Fall 2001): 281-290.

40. Davidson, 34.

41. Felts, op. cit.

42. Allaire Corporation, "ColdFusion 4,5 White Paper," 1999, Available: <http://www.allaire.com/Documents/Objects/WhitePaper/CF45WhitePaper.doc>. Accessed: December 15, 2001.

43. Daniel Cunliffe, "Developing Usable Web Sites–A Review and Model," *Internet Research: Electronic Applications and Policy* 10, no. 4 (2000): 295-307.

44. Sanjay Patel and Charles Linville, "Hot Searches with ColdFusion," *Web Techniques*, Available: <http://www.webtechniques.com/archives/2000/04/patel/>. Accessed: December 15, 2001.

45. Jeff Straathof, "Load Testing Intranet Applications: Finding Hidden Bottlenecks," *Web Techniques* (January 1997): 53-54.

46. University of Washington, Computing and Communications, "Web Authentication Service," Available: <http://www.washington.edu/computing/pubcookie/>. Accessed: December 15, 2001.

47. Fusebox, Inc. Available: <http://www.fusebox.org/>. Accessed: December 15, 2001.

48. Marcia J. Bates, "Indexing and Access for Digital Libraries and the Internet: Human, Database, and Domain Factors," *Journal of the American Society for Information Science* 49, no. 13 (November 1998): 1185-1205.

49. Debra S. Ketchell, Leilani St. Anna, Sherry Dodson, Sara Safranek, and Terry Ann Jankowski, "Knowledge resources: Finding answers to primary care questions," In: *Primary Care Informatics*, Norris et al., ed., Springer-Verlag: in press.

50. Ketchell, "Too Many Channels," 177.

OTHER RESOURCES

ColdFusion for Libraries Discussion List, Available: <http://faculty.washington.edu/bwestra/cflist.html>. Accessed: 2001, December 17.

Ben Forta, *The ColdFusion 4.0 Web Application Construction Kit*, Indianapolis, Indiana: Que, 1998.

Appalachian State University Libraries' Ask A Librarian: A Reference Service for ASU Students, Faculty, Staff, and Alumni

Thomas McMillan Grant Bennett

SUMMARY. As dynamic content is filling the Internet, so are choices for implementing this service/tool for Web developers. This article concentrates on one of the solutions that offers choices and tools in a single free package. Zope delivers Web-based content using a variety of sources and Internet connections. At Appalachian State University, Ask A Librarian <http://www.library.appstate.edu/reference/askref.html> concentrates on using Zope, the PostgreSQL database, e-mail, and the Web to offer patrons the opportunity to receive guidance from reference librarians while at a remote location. *[Article copies available for a fee from The Haworth Document Delivery Service: 1-800-HAWORTH. E-mail address: <getinfo@haworthpressinc.com> Website: <http://www.HaworthPress.com> © 2002 by The Haworth Press, Inc. All rights reserved.]*

KEYWORDS. Internet, Web, database-driven, open source

Thomas McMillan Grant Bennett (bennetttm@appstate.edu) is Computer Consultant III, Appalachian State University, Library, 325 College Street, Boone, NC 28608-2026.

[Haworth co-indexing entry note]: "Appalachian State University Libraries' Ask A Librarian: A Reference Service for ASU Students, Faculty, Staff, and Alumni." Bennett, Thomas McMillan Grant. Co-published simultaneously in *Internet Reference Services Quarterly* (The Haworth Information Press, an imprint of The Haworth Press, Inc.) Vol. 7, No. 1/2, 2002, pp. 89-98; and: *Database-Driven Web Sites* (ed: Kristin Antelman) The Haworth Information Press, an imprint of The Haworth Press, Inc., 2002, pp. 89-98. Single or multiple copies of this article are available for a fee from The Haworth Document Delivery Service [1-800-HAWORTH, 9:00 a.m. - 5:00 p.m. (EST). E-mail address: getinfo@haworthpressinc.com].

89

INTRODUCTION

*The significant problems we face cannot be solved at the same
level of thinking we were at when we created them*

–Albert Einstein

The Appalachian State University (ASU) libraries' Ask A Librarian
is a service provided by reference librarians so patrons can do research
from remote locations and have professional guidance rather than having to physically be in the library to seek assistance. This project,
AskRef, began when remote library services were beginning to populate the Internet. The "problem" we faced at the time was, "How can
ASU libraries provide a reference assistance service to patrons in remote locations as they do with patrons that are in the library building?"

The original solution was to provide an e-mail link on the Web site
that allowed patrons to contact a reference librarian. A group of reference librarians agreed to monitor and respond to these e-mails. Even
with the speed of e-mail, this was not sufficient enough to provide
immediate assistance especially for someone who did not have an
Internet Service Provider (ISP) with an e-mail account or was at a remote location that did not provide e-mail client capabilities on the
user's computer. A second solution began to develop in the structure
of online Web forms utilizing Python as a Common Gateway Interface
(CGI).[1]

"Python is an interpreted, interactive, object-oriented programming
language. It is often compared to Tcl, Perl, Scheme or Java."[2] This solution allowed the library to require certain fields of information from
the patron, and it allowed immediate submission to the librarian. The
Python script appended the information to a text file on a Windows NT
server and separated each submission with a line of asterisks. This was
suitable for the patron, who only saw a page telling him or her that the
submission was received, but it didn't allow the librarians easy sepa-
ration of the submissions or the ability to store the submissions in a
form that could provide usable statistics and other features such as
automatically adding the question to a FAQ page. During the design
phase of AskRef using Python, awareness of tools that utilized Python emerged in the form of the Z Object Publishing Environment
(Zope).

ZOPE

What Is Zope?

"Zope is an open source Web application server that can be used for managing Web site content, building intranets, and creating portals. Zope is built using the Python programming language."[3] Zope was a new experience in learning Web interaction for the programmer. Zope comes with site management tools, a Web server, a search engine, database connectivity, security and collaboration services, and more. Zope allows Web site content to connect to a database in a way that the programmer can directly utilize the Structured Query Language (SQL) rather than have to interpret the SQL through the extra syntax required by CGI scripts or Java. For example, you don't have to reconnect to the database for each transaction. This became the "new level of thinking" needed to provide a viable solution to the AskRef project.

Zope is an Object Oriented environment that utilizes a super set of the Hyper Text Markup Language (HTML) called Document Template Markup Language (DTML). It provides its own interface for DTML editing using a Web form on the Zope server, although other tools can be used for editing. One of the beauties of using an object-oriented environment is the ability to create an object once and use it in multiple pages with a DTML tag. For example, the list of reference librarians for an HTML Select List can be created as a DTML Document and inserted as a tag everywhere a drop down list of reference librarians is needed. Once an object is defined, inheritance can be utilized. With a defined object, the DTML tag for that object can be used in the current directory or any directory below it. This has saved a lot of redundant coding by creating lists in the root directory of the server and using tags in the child directories for lists such as all library employees, student supervisors, and so on. Zope uses a Database Adapter (DA) to connect to an external database. There are several choices of popular databases that are supported by Zope DAs including Oracle, Sybase, MySQL, PostgreSQL, Open Database Connectivity (ODBC),[4] and others. When AskRef with Zope began on a Windows NT Server, MySQL was chosen as the database component. After purchasing a new server with Linux, PostgreSQL was selected as the database to use with Zope.[5] The Web site was moved with one file, data.fs. The data.fs file is the one file where Zope keeps all of its documents.

The Database

Creating the database requires the programmer to consider who will be using the database and what fields of information will need to be entered by users. The programmer must consider how patrons will enter information, and how librarians will utilize it to respond. Table 1 shows the "askref" database table structure used at ASU.

Besides the fields on the form, there are other fields in the database: *id*, which is an auto incremented number used to make each record unique and for retrieving specific records; *date*, which is automatically filled by the Zope Server; *add2dun*, a Boolean field that defaults to 'f' for "No this record has not had a response sent to the submitter," which the responder is allowed to set to 't' by clicking on a button labeled "Add to Done" in the "My Page" view; *add2faq*, a Boolean field that defaults to 'f' for "No this record is not in the Frequently Asked Questions," which the responder is allowed to set to 't' by clicking on a button labeled "Add to FAQ" in the "My Page" view; *responder*, a field set from a drop down Select List of librarians on the "Responder Page" by clicking a button labeled "Set"; *answer*, a field which is set after the librarian chooses Reply from the "My Page" view and then presses a submit button on the form that allows an answer to be entered into the database.

TABLE 1

Field	Type	Length
id	int4 not null serial	4
date	timestamp	4
phone	varchar()	12
affiliation	varchar()	15
add2dun	bool	1
add2faq	bool	1
responder	varchar()	15
e-mail	varchar()	60
question	text	var
answer	text	var
submitter	varchar()	40
subject	varchar()	51

HOW ASK A LIBRARIAN WORKS

Ask A Librarian starts with a Web form the user completes. The fields in the form are Name, Telephone number, E-mail address, Affiliation with ASU, Subject, and Your Question. When the submit button is clicked, the data from the form is added to the database by the Zope Server to a PostgreSQL database. This preserves the data in a true database from which data can be dynamically extracted and published on the Web. The name, e-mail address, and affiliation with ASU fields on the form must be completed or the user will receive a message after clicking on the Submit button that the required field or fields are not complete. The user is then allowed to go back and fill in all required fields and resubmit the question. The user can click on the "Start Over" button to clear all fields of the form and begin again. After a user clicks on the submit button, an acknowledgement page is presented informing the user that the information has been received and a University librarian will be responding to the question. There is a link back to the Ask A Librarian form on the confirmation page.

The "Responder Page" is the librarian's starting point for answering the "Ask A Librarian" questions (see Figure 1). The "Responder Page" has links to all of the pages the librarian will be using. The "Responder Page" shows all of the fields of the database except for the *add2dun* field and the *answer* field because the questions have not been answered

FIGURE 1

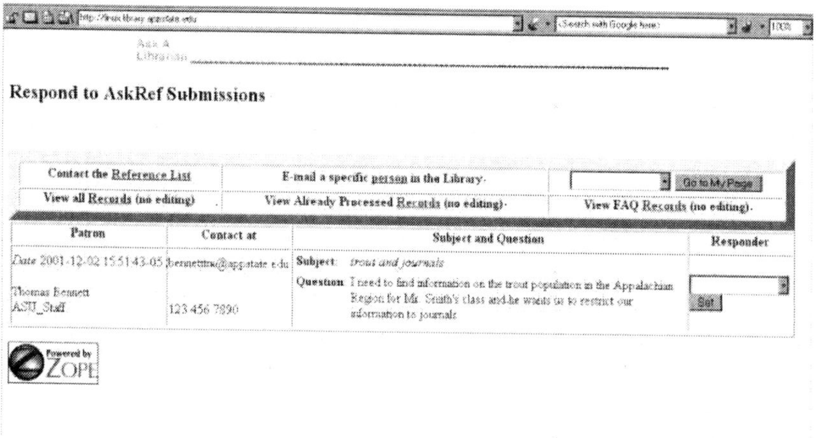

and are not yet assigned to a specific librarian. Near the top of this page is the choice of sending an e-mail to the reference listserv if the librarian wants to share this question with other librarians, clarify what is being asked, or request suggestions for responding. The next link at the top of the page is to the Library's Personnel Directory and allows the librarian to e-mail anyone in the library if additional information is needed to respond to the question. The third link in the top row lets the librarian bring up a Web page that will allow him or her to set an answer for the question, add the question to the Frequently Asked Questions Page, and/or set the page as Done. On the second row of links, the first lets you view all fields of all of the records in the database in descending order by date submitted. This view does not allow any editing and provides a link back to the "Responder Page." The second link on the second row lets you view only the questions that have been answered, or at least have been set to "have been answered" with no editing. The last link on the second row lets you view the FAQ page. There is no link back to the "Responder Page" from the FAQ page because this was planned to be a page available to the public. Currently, questions and answers have not been generic enough to utilize this feature although librarians are sending some questions to the FAQ for each other's reference.

The first step is to set the responder for each submission by choosing a name from the librarian drop down list. When a librarian is set as a responder, a confirmation page will indicate that the record is set for that librarian to respond. It is necessary to have a confirmation page for each question because of the nature of the database server; it won't allow you to stay on the same page. Once the user has set the submissions that he or she wishes to respond to, the user may then choose his or her name in the drop down menu and press the button labeled "Go To My Page." The librarian will then be at the "My Page" for "Ask A Librarian" which lists all the questions set for that librarian.

On the "My Page" for "Ask A Librarian" the choices are to go back to the "Responder Page," reply to a question, e-mail the answer to the submitter, add this question to the Done list, and/or add this question to the Frequently Asked Questions page (see Figure 2). The "Reply" button will bring up a form in the browser, where an answer can be added to the database. This does not send the answer to the person who submitted the question. The name of the person who submitted the question will appear in bright red to help verify it is the correct person. The question that was submitted is above the answer box. The answer box will automatically wrap text. Once the answer has been typed in, the responder presses the "Send Your Reply" button to add the answer to the database

FIGURE 2

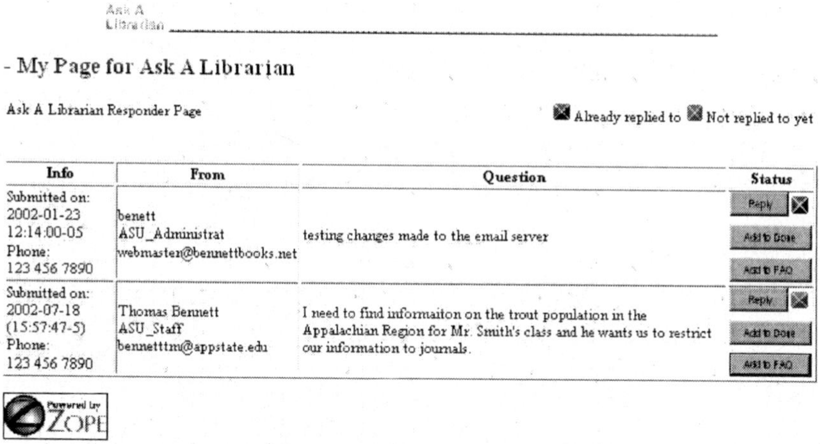

(see Figure 3). A dialog box will pop up requesting username and password to allow permission to e-mail a response (username and password can be attached to any object in Zope be it a folder, document, method [methods are documents that invoke actions], images, or any other type of object that can be defined in Zope). A new page will confirm that the answer is added to the database and the e-mail has been sent. Also, the librarian is copied in on the response so that he or she also receives the e-mail response. From that page the responder may choose to go back to the "My Page" page. On this page the responder may choose to add this question and answer to the "Frequently Asked Questions" page and/or set this question as Done. Once a question is set to Done it will only appear in the "View All Records" page and the "View Completed Questions" page. On "My Page" there is an icon beside the reply button that is blue if the question has not been answered and red if the question has been answered.

If the responder wants to add this record to the "Frequently Asked Questions" page, this must be done before clicking the "Add to Done" button. After clicking on the "Add to FAQ" button a confirmation page will appear indicating that this record has been added to the "Frequently Asked Questions" page and from that page the responder can go back to the "My Page" page or to the "Responder Page." Replacing the "Add to FAQ" button with the text of the question indicates that the record has been added to the "Frequently Asked Questions" page (see Figure 4).

FIGURE 3

recipient Thomas Bennett.

After clicking the "Send your reply" button, you will see a confirmation page stating that your message has been added to the database and the message has been emailed to Thomas Bennett. If you want this question added to the frequently asked questions use the page where you view all of the questions that you have not finished.

Subject:trout and journals

Question:I need to find informaiton on the trout population in the Appalachian Region for Mr. Smith's class and he wants us to restrict our information to journals.

```
A good beginning for finding resources on this would be...
Thank you for using AskRef
```

FIGURE 4

Ask A
Librarian

Frequently Asked Questions

Back to the Ask A Librarian Page.

 list or catalog of books on tape that are available for check out?

I was doing research in my room over the internet and I was trying to look up some articles under NC Live and it would not allow me to view any of them because I did not have a password. I was wondering if the library distributed this password so that student ant see research in cases such as this one. If so, please let me know what it is. Thanks, Alan

I need to find resources from after 1980 that concern maddness in Shakespeare's time and upon the plays of King Lear, Othello, Macbeth, Hamlet, and A Winter's Tale. Most of the resources I have found have been before 1980 or are unavailable. I would appriciate any information, online or textual. Thank you.

i have a term paper on sex workers or prostitutes in the early 20th century in america and why they were NOT powerless. Its suppose to be 6 pages long and i have only found like a paragraph of something usefull, where can i find more usefull info?

Where can I find journals about first amundment rights, freedom of speech, privacy act?

looking for Cole, E.B.& Stokes, J. St. Clair (1984). Caregiver-child interactive behaviors: A clinical procedure for the development of spoken language in hearing-impaired children. British Journal of Audiology, 18, 7-16. How to find and order. Thanks

I am looking for information about "communicative temptations" by Prizant, for fostering communication with very young language delayed children - tried searches unsuccessfully, but I know there is something out there. Thanks

Now the "Add to Done" button can be clicked to indicate that this record is finished. Again, a confirmation page will indicate that the record has been added to the processed records list and the librarian may go back to the "My Page" page, or to the "Responder Page."

The Frequently Asked Questions page is an HTML page with two rows where each row is a frame. The top frame consists of a title logo. The second frame is a scrollable list of questions. When the "Show Me" button is clicked, the question (for confirmation) and answer appear in a new page along with the date submitted and the contact person for that question. The contact person's name is a link to the Web Mailto page for that person where a patron may submit a form that will be e-mailed to that library employee.

CONCLUSION

Ask A Librarian had its debut at Appalachian State University in Spring Semester 2000 after several months of planning and developing a proper and practical solution to implement it. Ask A Librarian can be seen at <http://www.library.appstate.edu/Reference/askref.html>. ASU has received over 600 Ask A Librarian submissions since implementing the Zope server.

Zope is free to use and easy to install for Linux and Windows. There are compiled versions for other platforms and the source is available so it can also be compiled on other platforms. Several Zope users agree that the learning curve is steep at first, but once you catch on to its design this tool is an asset to any Webmaster or programmer. The choices of databases to use with Zope include the most popular commercial and open source tools. Specific choices include Oracle, Sybase, PostgreSQL, and MySQL among others. This integration of database and Web server allows a Web site to deliver dynamic Web content based on database queries and to collect information in a structure that lends itself to extensive manipulation. Zope has a simple Web user interface. There is only minor configuration needed when setting up a Zope Server. Being an open source product, it can be customized through its built-in tools or using Python scripts referred to as External Methods.

The members of Zope e-mail lists provide excellent assistance through their experiences. Several members of the lists have created "How-to" pages for Zope managers to access and utilize. As of February 2001, there were 10,500 Zope.org members, 2,700 Zope mailing list subscribers with 2,500 messages a month, and 87,000 Zope downloads from

January 2001 through the end of February 2001. Zope is a product developed by Digital Creations and is now known as the Zope Corporation.[6] Digital Creations decided to make Zope available as open source while they concentrated their commercial business in serving as consultants to Zope site developers.

Following are a couple of the comments offered by reference librarians in discussing the Zope implementation of Ask A Librarian:

> I really like how our AskRef is set up and, once you worked out a few initial bugs, I think it is really easy to use.

> I think the Zope database setup you created for us is excellent. It's straightforward and easy to use. It does just about everything we need it to–and not a lot more. I personally don't like using programs that have way too many features and get me confused. I like the fact that I can check for questions, or compose and send answers, from anywhere that I have Web access. The process of moving a question to my own page, thus indicating that it has been claimed and will be worked on, is really a smart solution for this team-based service. And being able to make a question "go away" from my page when I'm done with it is smart, too. I think you've produced a wonderful system for us; it's easy to use, and it serves us well!

NOTES

1. W3C documentation on CGI: <http://www.w3.org/CGI/>.

2. Documentation on Python: <http://www.python.org/doc/Summary.html>.

3. Documentation on Zope: <http://www.zope.org/Documentation/ZWN/ZWN-2001-10-01>.

4. Microsoft's home page for ODBC: <http://www.microsoft.com/data/odbc/>.

5. For a comparison of MySQL and PostgreSQL, see <http://www.phpbuilder.com/mail/php-general/2000102/2577.php>.

6. Documentation on the Zope Corporation: <http://www.zope.com/CaseStudies/> (these quotes change with each refresh of the pages).

Bibliographic Citation Management Software for Web Applications

Ann Koopman

SUMMARY. The bibliographic citation management software librarians already use to support scholarly research can also be used to deliver databases to the Web. Scott Memorial Library at Thomas Jefferson University uses a combination of Reference Manager and Reference Web Poster to publish indexes to bibliographic literature, and searchable lists of electronic journals and frequently asked questions (FAQs). This approach to serving data is suitable for materials of a bibliographic nature and/or for low budgets. To get started, all that is required is a copy of a citation management program, such as Reference Manager, EndNote, ProCite or Biblioscape. Any of these will produce static pages coded in HTML. Optional additional packages (Reference Web Poster or BiblioWeb Server) provide interactive Web-based searching. *[Article copies available for a fee from The Haworth Document Delivery Service: 1-800-HAWORTH. E-mail address: <getinfo@haworthpressinc.com> Website: <http://www. HaworthPress.com> © 2002 by The Haworth Press, Inc. All rights reserved.]*

KEYWORDS. Bibliographic citation management software, Web databases, Reference Web Poster, Reference Manager

INTRODUCTION

For several years, Thomas Jefferson University's Scott Memorial Library has supported the scholarly use of bibliographic citation manage-

---

Ann Koopman (Ann.Koopman@mail.tju.edu) is JEFFLINE Editor, Scott Memorial Library, Thomas Jefferson University, Philadelphia, PA.

[Haworth co-indexing entry note]: "Bibliographic Citation Management Software for Web Applications." Koopman, Ann. Co-published simultaneously in *Internet Reference Services Quarterly* (The Haworth Information Press, an imprint of The Haworth Press, Inc.) Vol. 7, No. 1/2, 2002, pp. 99-112; and: *Database-Driven Web Sites* (ed: Kristin Antelman) The Haworth Information Press, an imprint of The Haworth Press, Inc., 2002, pp. 99-112. Single or multiple copies of this article are available for a fee from The Haworth Document Delivery Service [1-800-HAWORTH, 9:00 a.m. - 5:00 p.m. (EST). E-mail address: getinfo@haworthpressinc. com].

99

ment software in conjunction with database searching. Faculty use it both individually and collaboratively to store references and to format bibliographies when they write articles. Some librarians also use it to manage their own collections of research materials. Librarians who were familiar with the software saw its potential for delivery of data to the Web over the course of several projects undertaken by the library. Please note that while the examples that follow are based on Jefferson's experiences with Reference Manager and Reference Web Poster, similar results can be achieved with other products, including Biblioscape/ BiblioWeb Server, EndNote and ProCite.

DHNet: MODEL FOR COLLABORATION

In 1995, the National Center for Dental Hygiene Research (NCDHR), then located at Jefferson, received a grant from the Bureau of Health Professions to support the training of dental hygienists in collaborative research methods. Included in the grant was support for a new index to dental hygiene research literature, which was to include reports of new and in-progress research projects undertaken by the research teams. The library participated by developing a controlled vocabulary for the field and by establishing the format of descriptive records. Researchers were to be responsible for populating the database with descriptions of their work, through submission of Web-based forms. The library also constructed a Web presence for this dental hygiene network, called DHNet <http://jeffline.tju.edu/DHNet/>.

The first version of the DHNet database was constructed using Oracle, that being the database software used by local university programmers. Such an arrangement, however, was quite cumbersome and expensive. It was also overkill for a small bibliographic project. As part of the research training provided by the grant, hygienists were already learning how to use Reference Manager software, so they were familiar with its appearance, and NCDHR staff were familiar with its operation. When the companion Reference Web Poster program became available, it was quickly recognized as an ideal solution for the DHNet knowledgebase. Reference Manager's bibliographic database was fully equipped to accept the type of descriptive information needed by DHNet, while Web Poster provided immediate, interactive, field-based search capability.

First, the records were moved from Oracle to a Reference Manager database. Then the Reference Manager database was loaded on Web

Poster for delivery to the Web. Researchers still submitted new information or updates using simple Web-based forms, for review by NCDHR staff before addition to the knowledgebase. Because Reference Manager had an active URL field, the DHNet records could link to full-text descriptions of research projects, images, or any articles the NCDHR had copyright permission to mount. Web Poster allowed some customization of a descriptive paragraph at the top of the search form, along with some search and display preferences.

Simple and advanced search interfaces are available on Web Poster <http://jeffit.tju.edu/RIS/RISWEB.ISA>. The quick search option allows the user to choose any of up to 10 databases, and searches the author, keyword, periodical title, and publication date fields. Boolean operators are supported, and searched terms are highlighted in the retrieved results. Retrieval screens provide short display and full display of records, with options to mark records for download. Users may download from the database directly into any other ISI ResearchSoft product, or in other formats that can, in turn, be imported into other types of databases.

The advanced search option features field-based searching in specified fields, such as authors or periodical name, and multi-field searching (see Figure 1). Records are retrieved and displayed in brief format, according to a selected bibliographic style. Full records are linked from the brief records. Note that field labels have been customized and a URL links to the full text of a paper in Figure 2.

The Reference Web Poster product is extremely simple to install and operate–it uses only three screens. It is available for Windows environments, and makes use of separate Web server software installed on the same machine. Since personal Web servers are already included as part of the operating system on most new PCs, this is a good solution for small projects. Other server types are supported for more substantial projects; for example, Jefferson uses Windows 2000 with an IIS server. The program even tracks some basic use statistics. The software allows an administrator to make choices, such as how many records may be retrieved in a single search, whether to include custom language at the top of the page, and which databases to make available, among others.

Web Poster accepts databases from EndNote, ProCite, and Reference Manager, all of which are ISI ResearchSoft products. Other companies do compete in this market, however. The BiblioWeb Server, for example, is based on Biblioscape citation management software. Features common to both include:

- field-based search options for users.
- record field customization options for the database producer (e.g., to include or exclude fields, rename existing fields, or add custom fields).
- support for non-English language and scientific characters.
- marking and downloading options for users.

While Web Poster supports only search and view activity, the BiblioWeb software allows a database producer to authenticate users, thereby allowing them to add material online to the live database. Both Biblioscape <http://www.biblioscape.com> and ISI ResearchSoft <http://www. isiresearchsoft.com> provide substantial product information and trial software on their Web sites.

FIGURE 1. The Advanced Search Interface

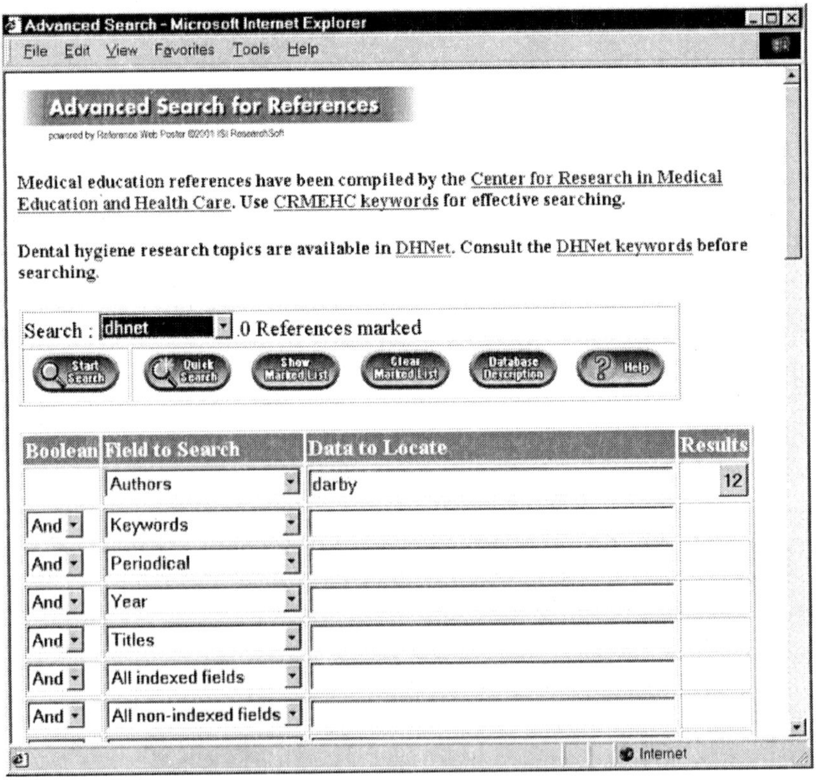

FIGURE 2. A Full DHNet Record

Reference 1 of 12 Marked

Database	: dhnet
Ref Type	: Research in Progress
Ref ID	: 12
Title	: The Cultural Adaptability of Dental Hygiene, Medical Laboratory Sciences, Nursing, and Physical Therapy Faculty
Authors of Book	: Connolly,Irene; ***Darby,Michele L.***; Smith,Dawn; Thomson-Lakey,Evelyn; Tolle-Watts,Lynn;
Date Review Published	: Wednesday, July 01, 1998
Web/URL	: http://jeffline.tju.edu/DHNet/papers/dhn_paper126.html
Keywords	: Cultural norms and values; Faculty; Descriptive research; Socialization theory;
Abstract	: The Cross-Cultural Adaptability Inventory (Kelley and Meyers, 1992) was used to measure the cross-cultural adaptability of the dental hygiene, medical laboratory sciences, nursing and physical therapy faculty at Old Dominion University, Norfolk, Virginia. Results of the 40 full-time faculty surveyed revealed that the health sciences faculty possess similar levels of cross-cultural adaptability and that these levels are slightly higher than a norm group possessing culturally sensitive skills. Results suggest that the majority of the health science faculty possess qualities necessary to be cross-culturally adaptable. (Abstract by research team)
Research Design	: Descriptive
Theoretical Framework	: Socialization Theory
Test Instrument	: Cross-Cultural Adaptability Inventory
Financial Sponsor	: American Dental Hygienists Association
Author's Keywords	: Cultural Adaptability

The DHNet continued for several years as a model project for collaborative research. The project was presented at several professional meetings and was described in print.[1] The National Center for Dental Hygiene Research is currently located at the University of Southern California.

CRMEHC: ANOTHER SEARCHABLE INDEX

A similar application, encompassing citations to bibliographic literature, was the result of another externally-funded study. With support from the federal Health Resources and Services Administration, Jefferson's Center for Research in Medical Education and Health Care (CRMEHC) compiled a bibliography spanning four decades of research on physician work force analysis, primary care, managed care, and the cost of medical education.[2-4] Dissemination of the bibliography to other researchers was an important condition stipulated in the grant. Before the advent of the Web, the CRMEHC would have published its index in book form, with limited distribution. As this project continues to grow, using Reference Manager and Reference Web Poster, updates become available without the cost of a print publication, and the resource is freely available to all Internet users <http://jeffline.tju.edu/CWIS/crmehc/publications.htm>.

Reference Manager is used to accumulate the data, using custom fields and standard record types. The library has only one server available for this project and only one copy of Web Poster to support both CRMEHC and DHNet. Users may search each database individually, or both together. This has been disconcerting to some users, but the approach is one librarians encounter daily. When reminded, most users do realize they are familiar with aggregators like OVID, SilverPlatter, or Dialog, where searchers must choose among disparate databases that share a single unifying search interface. Note that the fields contained in an individual database record may differ from database to database (compare Figures 2 and 3), and the contents of fields can be structured in a variety of ways.

Because the CRMEHC index is an ongoing project, the database is updated regularly with new material. Web Poster, however, only works with a static database. Whenever the CRMEHC indexer needs to update the online database, the Reference Manager file is copied, added to Web

FIGURE 3. A Full CRMEHC Record

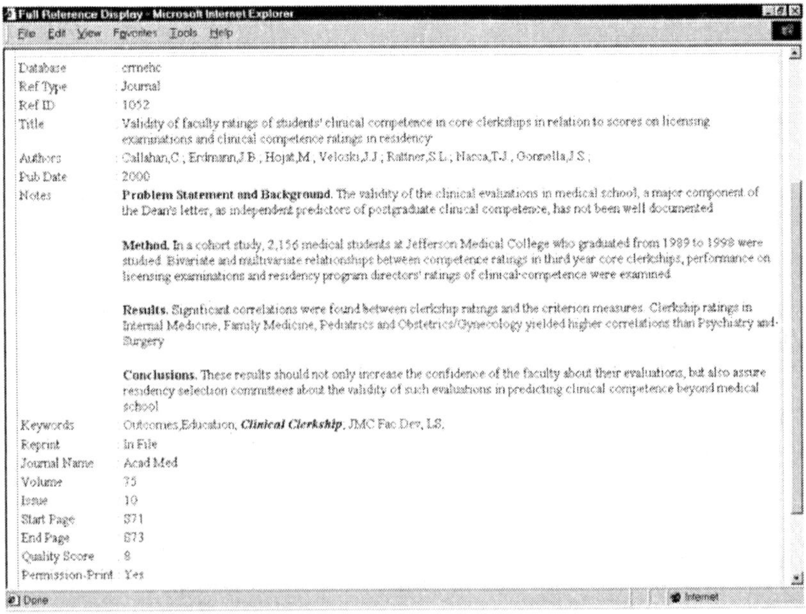

Poster, and the outdated copy is removed. By contrast, BiblioWeb works with a live file online, so authenticated users may update it with new material or make changes to existing material in real time. An application of BiblioWeb is viewable at the University of Pennsylvania's Southeast Asian Archaeology Scholarly Website <http://seasia.museum. upenn.edu/>.

E-JOURNAL LISTS

While it remains the library's goal to use our online catalog as the source from which to derive secondary representations of materials such as an electronic journal page, it will be some time before this can be realized. In the meantime, users expect the convenience of an electronic journal list outside of the catalog. User expectation is so strong that, for the short term, the library maintains a parallel database for materials in electronic format. Unfortunately, Web Poster is not an appropriate tool to deliver a journal title database. Search fields in Web Poster's advanced search interface cannot be customized or deleted, so users would be confused by an option to search by author, for example, in a list of journal titles. In this case, the ability of any citation management software package to customize its output turned out to be the key.

Years ago, the library started to list electronic journals with a simple hand-coded file, using frames. Journals were grouped alphabetically, with icons to click for descriptive information. That was adequate for a very small collection. However, when the collection started to grow rapidly, it became quite time-consuming to maintain. The introduction of proxy services made it clear that technical staff required a database for adequate control of subscription status and proxy server permissions. Since a database was needed for these internal management purposes, it also made sense to use it as a source from which to derive the online journal lists. A bibliographic citation managements program was chosen because of its built-in bibliographic structure, and because staff were already familiar with its use. Delivery models were developed from the database, taking into account end-user criticisms of the old design: frames were unpopular, users had to take initiative to click for descriptive information, and the pictorial icons did not convey enough meaning. More than any other feature, the ability to search by title keyword was desired by users.

Library staff also needed special fields in addition to standard bibliographic information, such as information required by the proxy server (see Figure 4). The database was also adapted to include records for other materials managed by the proxy server, such as databases, books, and instructional software, in addition to the electronic journals. Reference Manager allows extensive customization of a bibliographic database, with multiple optional fields, field naming options, and choice of whether to include any of the 35 different profiles available to describe different types of records. Each citation management product differs in the number of record types, fields per record, and customizability of fields. While the allowed number of reference types and fields is generous in all of the software packages, one of the limitations of using bibliographic citation management software is that there *are* limits. None of the products offers infinite expandability of fields.

The search and retrieval features of citation management software allow a database producer to limit the output to selected records and to selected fields of records. For example, the technical support information that would not be suitable for public display can be excluded, or only records that meet specified conditions can be included. In this way, a single database can support multiple types of materials and demands.

FIGURE 4. Staff View of an Electronic Journal Record in Reference Manager

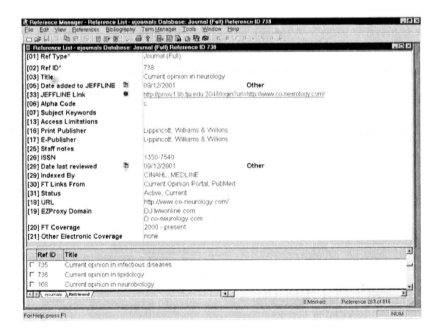

Jefferson generates two types of lists:

1. a tabular-style file, for use in an HTML template (see Figure 5), and
2. a paragraph-style file, for use with a UNIX shell script to support simple keyword searches (see Figure 6).

Both are static files, with HTML tags added to the content of the database fields by Reference Manager as part of a custom output style. While Reference Manager itself must run on a Windows platform, the text files derived from Reference Manager can be used in any server environment, including the main library UNIX server.

To produce lists in a format suitable for insertion into a basic template, Reference Manager provides an output style wizard. In effect, each type of output is considered a bibliographic style. Just as one would produce a reference list for an article to be published in *JAMA*, one can produce a table or paragraph of descriptive journal data to be

FIGURE 5. Public View of the Electronic Journal List, in Tabular Style

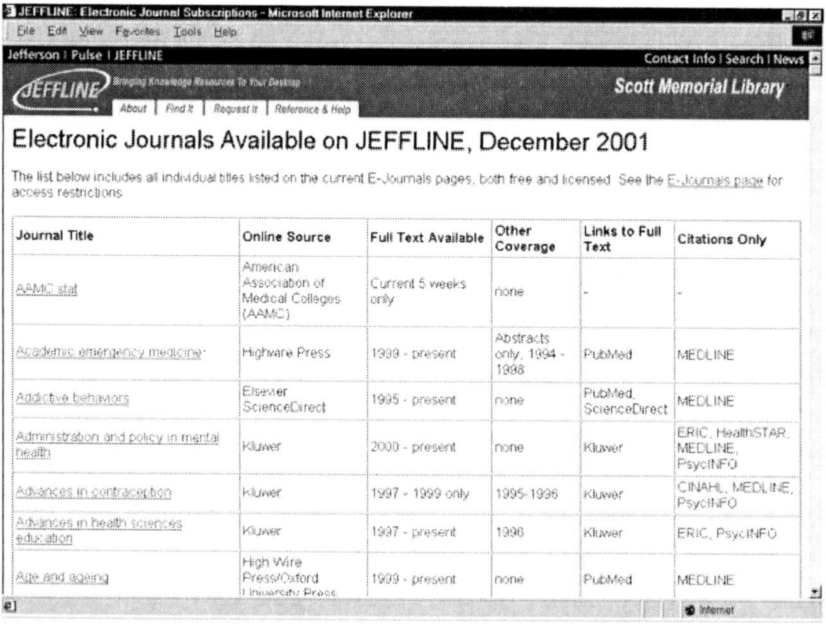
JEFFLINE: Electronic Journal Subscriptions - Microsoft Internet Explorer

File Edit View Favorites Tools Help

Jefferson | Pulse | JEFFLINE   Contact Info | Search | News

JEFFLINE   Scott Memorial Library

About | Find It | Request It | Reference & Help

Electronic Journals Available on JEFFLINE, December 2001

The list below includes all individual titles listed on the current E-Journals pages, both free and licensed. See the E-Journals page for access restrictions.

Journal Title	Online Source	Full Text Available	Other Coverage	Links to Full Text	Citations Only
AAMC stat	American Association of Medical Colleges (AAMC)	Current 5 weeks only	none	-	-
Academic emergency medicine*	Highwire Press	1999 - present	Abstracts only, 1994 - 1998	PubMed	MEDLINE
Addictive behaviors	Elsevier ScienceDirect	1995 - present	none	PubMed, ScienceDirect	MEDLINE
Administration and policy in mental health	Kluwer	2000 - present	none	Kluwer	ERIC, HealthSTAR, MEDLINE, PsycINFO
Advances in contraception	Kluwer	1997 - 1999 only	1995-1996	Kluwer	CINAHL, MEDLINE, PsycINFO
Advances in health sciences education	Kluwer	1997 - present	1996	Kluwer	ERIC, PsycINFO
Age and ageing	High Wire Press/Oxford University Press	1999 - present	none	PubMed	MEDLINE

Internet

FIGURE 6. The Search Results Screen, in Paragraph Style

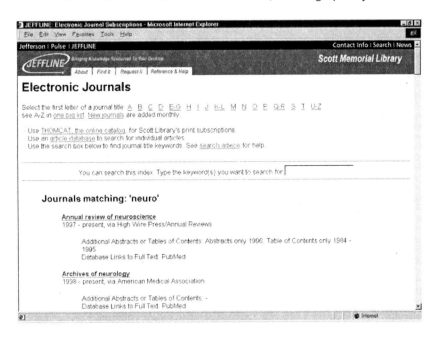

published on a Web page. Custom styles allow a user to choose text to precede or follow database field elements in output. Such text can include HTML coding tags. For example, a URL field can be attached to a title in order to make the title clickable as a regular link on a Web page. The style format used to create the table presentation shown in Figure 5 is shown in Figure 7. The output takes the form of a text file, which may then be inserted directly into a page template, or stored as a separate text file and called into the template as needed.

Jefferson's tabular pages use separate text files, which are called into a template with a server side include command. A page template can consist of any header, footer, or side materials. A server side include, such as <!–#include file="ejls.txt"–>, is used to call the text file into the template. Using this technique, the content of the list can be used by several different templates as needed. For example, as the library explores the needs of PDA users for smaller screen displays, the ability to make content flexible is increasingly important.

Alphabetical lists are important, but users also requested keyword search capability for journals' titles and publishers. Because these files

FIGURE 7. Reference Manager's Output Wizard

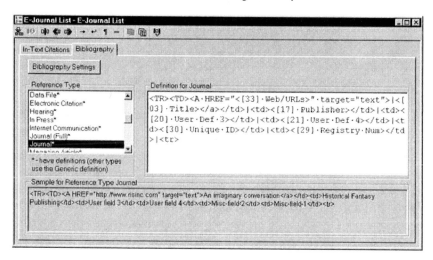

are housed on a UNIX server, keyword searching is possible using a UNIX shell script to search text output from the Reference Manager database. The text file is again the result of a custom output style, which wraps HTML tags around database field content, producing output such as:

```
<p><a

href="http://proxy1.lib.tju.edu:2048/login?url=http://www.catchword.com

/rpsv/cw/guilford/08999546/contp1.htm" target="new"><strong>AIDS

education and prevention</strong></a><br>2001 - present, via Catchword

<blockquote>Additional Abstracts or Tables of Contents: - <br>Database

Links to Full Text: PubMed</blockquote>
```

The result is a paragraph presentation, as preferred by users (see Figure 6). The script searches for any string of characters in the title or description of the journal, but is not field-based, and does not have Boolean or logical truncation options. For more sophisticated types of searches, users are referred to the online catalog.

Searches can be defined by user or preset by librarians. The preset queries are used to answer frequently asked questions or to generate handouts. An example of a preset search is a query for all journals in the library's collection whose full-text articles are available via PubMed LinkOut. For such popular requests, a link is provided on the electronic journals page, incorporating the search request in the link. Copies of the scripts used by Jefferson are freely available from the author, upon request.

While it might seem to be a lot of work to generate the text files, most of the time and effort is actually in the planning and original layout design of the templates and output definitions. Once those are in place, the bulk of maintenance time lies in tracking the journal subscription information. Production of the page updates can be done with minimal effort by trained technical staff. Scott Library regenerates pages whenever journal subscription changes occur, usually on a monthly basis. Once database entries have been updated, the actual generation of new pages takes less than 15 minutes.

A Reference Manager database holds unlimited references, up to 10 databases may be mounted on a single instance of Reference Web Poster, and the program can reliably support many simultaneous users (at least 30, in TJU's experience). BiblioWeb Server advertises a capacity to support hundreds of simultaneous users. Of course, the capability of the server affects performance. A small personal computer running Personal Web server obviously will not support the same level of service as a more sophisticated server. An electronic journals list is usually one of the most heavily-hit areas of a library's site, so it is important to match the capacity of the server to demand. At the same time, most users do not linger on the title lists; they look for something and quickly move on.

FREQUENTLY ASKED QUESTIONS (FAQS)

In addition to bibliographic material and serials control, librarians at TJU have experimented with Reference Manager for delivery of a searchable FAQ list. Again, because Web Poster's Advanced Search fields are not customizable, a text file and cgi script are used to generate the FAQ. These work in exactly the same manner as the electronic journals list.

CONCLUSION

It is possible to do quite a lot with small tools. If access to database programmers is a problem, or tools like ColdFusion or PHP are not available, then consider how far you can get, armed only with a personal computer and citation management software. Such a solution may be all a small library needs, or it may fill a gap until the local library catalog develops stronger capabilities. The bibliographic nature of the software also provides immediate support for certain faculty publishing needs.

Consider the criteria in Table 1 when deciding whether to try citation management tools for delivery of Web materials.

TABLE 1. Criteria for Evaluation of Citation Management Tools

Issue	Interactive Presentation*	Static Presentation**
Material to be included is bibliographic in nature	Yes	Yes
Links to external electronic objects are required	Yes	Yes
Windows/NT server is available	Yes, limited to Windows/NT server	Yes, any type of server may be used
User may search for individual records	Yes, built in	No, requires custom script programming (cgi, Perl)
User may download individual records	Yes	No
Database does not contain the descriptive fields listed in the Reference Web Poster or BiblioWeb search box	No, search fields cannot be customized	Yes, custom output allows selective display
Special Web display format is required	No, display format is fixed	Yes, display format can be manipulated
Record fields include both public and internal information	No, all fields are displayed automatically	Yes, fields may be selected for inclusion or exclusion

* Interactive presentation via Reference Web Poster or BiblioWeb Server.
** Static presentation via HTML derived from any citation management software.

NOTES

1. J. L. Forrest and A. E. Koopman, "DHNet: A Model for International Research Collaboration," *Journal of Allied Health* 27, no. 1 (Winter 1998): 39-44 (Proceedings from the Second Annual World Congress on Allied Health, Telford, England, July 23, 1997).

2. C. J. Martini, J. J. Veloski, B. Barzansky, G. Xu, and S. K. Fields, "Medical School and Student Characteristics that Influence Choosing a Generalist Career," *JAMA* 272, no. 9 (September 7, 1994): 661-668.

3. J. J. Veloski, B. Barzansky, D. B. Nash, S. Bastacky, and D. P. Stevens, "Medical Student Education in Managed Care Settings: Beyond HMOs," *JAMA* 276, no. 9 (September 4, 1996): 667-671.

4. J. R. Boex, A. A. Boll, L. Franzini et al., "Measuring the Costs of Primary Care Education in the Ambulatory Setting," *Academic Medicine* 75, no. 5 (May 2000): 419-425.

Databases to the Web:
From Static to Dynamic on the Express

Mary Platt

SUMMARY. The need to deliver current data on periodical holdings and electronic resources led the staff at Kennesaw State University's Sturgis Library to develop database-driven dynamic Web pages. The project's success was based on the incorporation of skills, technologies and hardware that were already in place in the library with Allaire's ColdFusion Express, a free, feature-limited version of ColdFusion Web application server. *[Article copies available for a fee from The Haworth Document Delivery Service: 1-800-HAWORTH. E-mail address: <getinfo@ haworthpressinc.com> Website: <http://www.HaworthPress.com> © 2002 by The Haworth Press, Inc. All rights reserved.]*

KEYWORDS. ColdFusion, database-driven Web sites

INTRODUCTION

Like most libraries, Sturgis Library at Kennesaw State University (KSU) <http://www.kennesaw.edu/library> has struggled over the past decade with the problem of efficiently delivering current information

---

Mary Platt (mplatt@kennesaw.edu) is Assistant Librarian, Coordinator of Electronic Resources, Sturgis Library, Kennesaw State University, 1000 Chastain Road, Kennesaw, GA 30144.

[Haworth co-indexing entry note]: "Databases to the Web: From Static to Dynamic on the Express." Platt, Mary. Co-published simultaneously in *Internet Reference Services Quarterly* (The Haworth Information Press, an imprint of The Haworth Press, Inc.) Vol. 7, No. 1/2, 2002, pp. 113-121; and: *Database-Driven Web Sites* (ed: Kristin Antelman) The Haworth Information Press, an imprint of The Haworth Press, Inc., 2002, pp. 113-121. Single or multiple copies of this article are available for a fee from The Haworth Document Delivery Service [1-800-HAWORTH, 9:00 a.m. - 5:00 p.m. (EST). E-mail address: getinfo@haworthpressinc. com].

113

about its resources, beyond the library catalog, to patrons. Neither periodicals nor electronic resources were being cataloged in KSU's OPAC, and patrons, including a student body of nearly 14,000, needed to know what Sturgis Library had and how to get it. By the mid-1990s the Web was the obvious preference over hard copy lists to deliver this information, and patrons soon expected it to be there. Though the need was filled for a time with static lists on the library's home pages, these were as time consuming to maintain, if not more so, as paper lists. Using database-driven Web pages delivering dynamic content became a possible solution worth exploring for making this periodical and electronic resources information available to both local and remote patrons.

EXPLORING THE OPTIONS

Various methods of creating database-driven Web pages were being discussed in the literature,[1,2] at conferences [3] and on listservs over the next few years. Although any solution would certainly mean developing new skills and introducing new technologies to staff in Sturgis Library, one that presented minimal obstacles had to be found. The library has no technology professional among its staff of 28 full-time employees, and at that time relied only on the campus Web server, where the library had an allocation of space for static pages, for delivery of its Web pages. Any fulfillment of the dynamic Web page dream had to come from in-house ingenuity.

Some solutions involved software that was expensive and too costly to allow staff to explore its potential for use at KSU. Other solutions involved programming skills, such as ASP, Perl and CGI, that would take time to develop and that would require expanded coordination and access into the campus Web server. Some solutions involved migrating the existing data into new database management software, like MySQL, that would be unfamiliar to the staff maintaining it. The open-source solutions using PHP and Linux, for example, with which many libraries have had success recently were not yet widely available (if at all) and would require, again, time to develop the technical background to install and manipulate a new operating system, programming skills and, more importantly, spare hardware on which to experiment.

Over the course of several years, Allaire's ColdFusion came to light as the software choice of many library Web developers for dynamic Web pages.[4] It could be used on a Windows platform, which is the standard for Sturgis Library and KSU, and with Microsoft Access, which most of the staff were already using. Some of the data for the proposed pages at KSU were already being maintained in Access. And as Harker[5] notes, ColdFusion is "easy enough for development work by relatively unsophisticated 'application developers,' " and the markup language (CFML) would not be difficult to master by anyone with a basic understanding of HTML, which was also an existing skill set among the staff at Sturgis Library. An online course through ZDU-Ziff Davis (now Element K, <http://www.elementk.com>) provided the Coordinator of Electronic Resources the opportunity for hands-on experience with ColdFusion at the desktop PC before any further commitment of funds, training or resources needed to be made.

THE ONLINE TRAINING

A prerequisite to the ColdFusion course was one on Structured Query Language (SQL) to learn the logic and the structure of creating the select statements that would be integral to ColdFusion scripting. This also added insight into database design and structure that would prove helpful with the library projects.

The ColdFusion course used ColdFusion Express <http://www.macromedia.com/software/coldfusion/trial/cf_server_express.html>, the free, limited functionality version of the Web server application software; it also used Microsoft Access databases and an evaluation version of Allaire's Homesite for writing HTML and CFML. The Level 1 course covered the entire process of installing and configuring a personal Web server and the ColdFusion software on the PC, using the ColdFusion tags to develop an array of basic dynamic applications, and designing query (<CFQUERY>) and output (<CFOUTPUT>) statements to achieve a variety of results. Support, advice and inspiration were found (and still are) through CFVault: The Allaire Information Source <http://www.cfvault.com>, Webmonkey <http://hotwired.lycos.com/webmonkey/programming/coldfusion/index.html>, and particularly from the ColdFusion for Libraries listserv <http://faculty.washington.edu/bwestra/cflist.html>. With this preview of the potential of ColdFusion for Sturgis Library, the vision of dynamic database-driven Web pages was finally pulled off the back burner.

BRINGING THE DYNAMIC PAGES TO LIFE

The periodical holdings data, which initially included title, format, location and coverage dates, had been compiled in a WordPerfect file and maintained in Technical Services by serials staff for internal use and to provide Public Services with a printed list of periodical holdings several times a year. From the beginning, the list integrated print and electronic full-text titles from journal aggregators, then eventually individual e-journal subscriptions; staff realized that patrons' needs were not defined by format, and that they would need all titles, regardless of format, presented in one document. The list then was converted to Microsoft Word with active hyperlinks to the online titles to generate static HTML Web pages that displayed holdings through the library home pages. Students could now access the information from anywhere on campus or from home and make the online link to the full-text article where it was available.

As the project to move to database-driven pages evolved, the data in the Word file was carefully tab-delimited and pulled into Microsoft Access. Additional data such as subject and language coding were added to the database. Considerable time and attention were given at this time to configuring the Access database with appropriate tables, field properties and links to give flexibility to the search and display capabilities of the final dynamic Web pages. Accommodating titles with online access in more than one Web service, for example, required much trial and error to successfully display the correct URL to the second Web service. Page design itself presented challenges; frames and tables were used to allow column headers, which include links to necessary location details, to align with columns and remain visible as the pages were scrolled.

The electronic resources database was created in the early 1990s as an Access file by the Coordinator of Electronic Resources and had developed over the years with the information collected in the process of managing these resources. The file included data such as coverage, updates, subject, passwords, content descriptions, access locations, vendor and format on the electronic or digital information products that came to Sturgis Library. Again, all formats, including CD-ROMs, LAN, Internet and Web services, were integrated into one listing. This database was also used to generate a printed list used primarily at the Reference Desk to enable patrons to know what electronic products were available, how and where to access each title, and to give a brief description or scope note about each resource. Soon, the database was also used to create static Web pages using Access's "publish to the Web" function to deliver these details, as well as active links, to remote users.

Once the Element K online courses were completed, some of the course projects were modified as templates for Sturgis Library's real-life library needs, and the dynamic pages finally began to take shape. In order to deliver the new pages to KSU's patrons, an underused NT 4 server in the library was pulled into a new role as the library Web and database server by installing Microsoft Internet Information Server (IIS), ColdFusion Express, ODBC drivers, and both the periodical holdings and the electronic resources databases. This gave the option to manage the dynamic pages from the library's own server while continuing to use the campus server for static pages.

A uniform layout that relied heavily on the ColdFusion <CFINCLUDE> function (analogous to the server-side include) was designed for the pages and insured that any style changes needed would be easy to manage by modifying only the templates. Subject headings were reviewed and coordinated for use in both databases. And a system of maintaining the databases and updating them on the server was developed: serials staff in Technical Services still keep the periodical holdings data current in Access, and every 4-6 weeks this database as well as the electronic resources database are moved to the server to replace the old files. Quick fixes can be done by the Coordinator of Electronic Resources to correct immediate problems in the databases directly on the server. Both databases continue to be used for internal purposes in addition to feeding the dynamic Web pages. The electronic resources database now contains over 350 active records and the periodical holdings database over 3700.

EXPANDING SERVICES WITH DYNAMIC PAGES

As skills with ColdFusion grew and as new ways of extracting desired information from the databases and displaying it effectively became apparent, the pages have evolved. Both the Periodical Holdings (see Figure 1) <http://librarycentral.kennesaw.edu/cfdocs/jrnlsfrm.htm> and the Electronic Resources (see Figure 2) <http://librarycentral.kennesaw.edu/cfdocs/dbslistfrm.htm> pages in their latest versions have a subject search option, and the Periodical Holdings pages have language search capability, making them both truly interactive. Patrons can now select periodicals in the language of their choice, an option of-

FIGURE 1

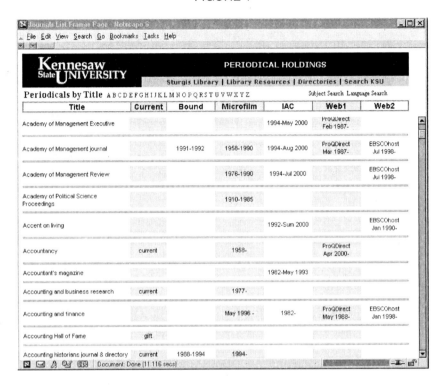

ten requested by foreign language students and international students. And they can limit lists of both periodicals and electronic resources to collections in their desired subjects.

With extensive use of the form and action pages and conditional logic functions, <CFIF> and <CFELSE>, the Electronic Resources pages are now able to present the users with resource-specific information such as off-campus access details that include the appropriate links and passwords or login instructions. Students now can find immediate answers to their oft-asked question, "Can I get this from home?" and "What's the password?"

An offshoot of the Periodical Holdings page is one that pulls from the same database a list of the newspaper holdings <http://librarycentral. kennesaw.edu/cfdocs/newspapers.cfm>. It was created to replace a popular existing static page where students can access a newspaper's home page as well as any full-text option available at KSU.

FIGURE 2

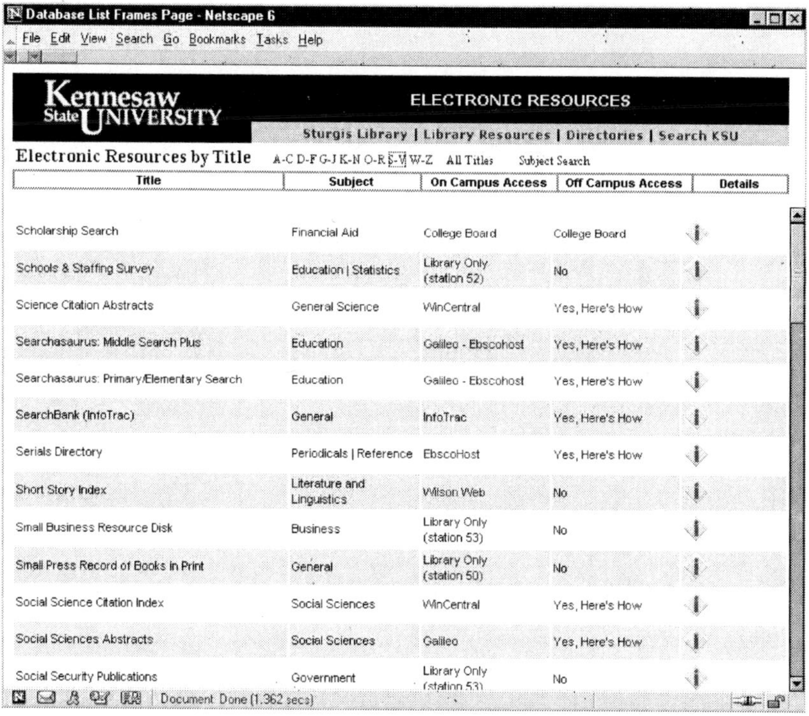
Database List Frames Page - Netscape 6

File Edit View Search Go Bookmarks Tasks Help

Kennesaw State UNIVERSITY

ELECTRONIC RESOURCES

Sturgis Library | Library Resources | Directories | Search KSU

Electronic Resources by Title A-C D-F G-J K-N O-R S-V W-Z All Titles Subject Search

Title	Subject	On Campus Access	Off Campus Access	Details
Scholarship Search	Financial Aid	College Board	College Board	
Schools & Staffing Survey	Education | Statistics	Library Only (station 52)	No	
Science Citation Abstracts	General Science	WinCentral	Yes, Here's How	
Searchasaurus: Middle Search Plus	Education	Galileo - Ebscohost	Yes, Here's How	
Searchasaurus: Primary/Elementary Search	Education	Galileo - Ebscohost	Yes, Here's How	
SearchBank (InfoTrac)	General	InfoTrac	Yes, Here's How	
Serials Directory	Periodicals | Reference	EbscoHost	Yes, Here's How	
Short Story Index	Literature and Linguistics	Wilson Web	No	
Small Business Resource Disk	Business	Library Only (station 53)	No	
Small Press Record of Books in Print	General	Library Only (station 50)	No	
Social Science Citation Index	Social Sciences	WinCentral	Yes, Here's How	
Social Sciences Abstracts	Social Sciences	Galileo	Yes, Here's How	
Social Security Publications	Government	Library Only (station 53)	No	

Document: Done (1.362 secs)

A third dynamic Web page project became possible with the discovery of the ease by which ColdFusion allows a Web user, in this case Sturgis Library staff, to update, insert and delete records in a database. Staff members have developed their own lists of favorite Web sites (free, non-subscription), particularly in areas of their subject expertise, and often faculty will recommend that their selections be made available to students through library Web pages as well. To alleviate the problem of multiple lists of Web sites, often with duplications, on the library home pages, an effort has been made to consolidate them into one subject-indexed collection. And in order to facilitate and encourage input from all library staff and to relieve any one person from the burden of all the maintenance, the Selected Web Sites page <http://librarycentral.kennesaw.edu/cfdocs/websearchfrm.htm> was designed so that staff can create and edit listings directly into the database on the server and select the appropriate subject headings from a secured Web form (see Figure 3). Each entry immediately becomes available on the Web site. Through these pages, students can access a fluid collection of links that is easily modified to reflect, for example, current campus-wide projects or community interests, as well as course-related sites.

CONCLUSION

All of these projects were completed and have performed exceptionally well using only ColdFusion Express, MS Access and Homesite (or NoteTab Light). And ColdFusion's ability to integrate with Dreamweaver, used by most of the library's Web authors, has streamlined a recent project to standardize library Web page header design to conform to new campus-wide guidelines.

Sturgis Library recently has purchased ColdFusion's development tool, Studio, and the Professional edition of ColdFusion Web server for its expanded functionality over Express, such as its support for table

FIGURE 3

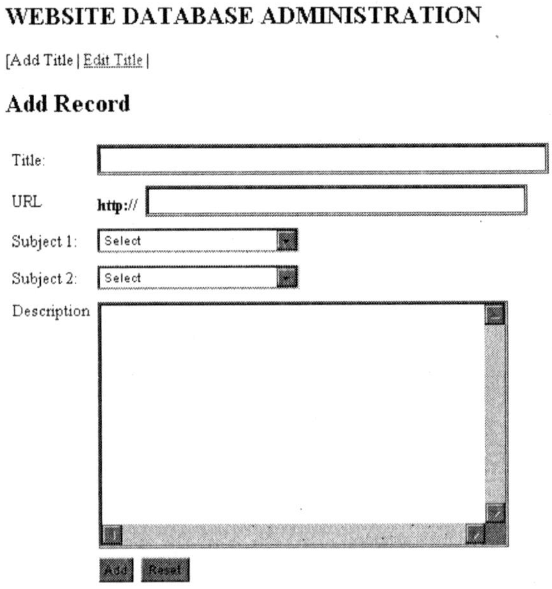

WEBSITE DATABASE ADMINISTRATION

[Add Title | Edit Title |

Add Record

Title:

URL   **http://**

Subject 1: Select

Subject 2: Select

Description

management and user authentication. With these and with new hardware and operating system options, we have plans to create applications that, among other things, will dynamically generate subject or pathfinder pages and listings of new books and resources by combining data from these existing databases with data extracted from the tables in the library's new Voyager catalog system and incorporating links to Sturgis Library's rapidly growing collection of electronic books.

The projects created with Access and Express may not be the final solution to the problem of effectively presenting current and accurate information about these ever-changing resources to KSU's users, but they are low-budget and within the scope of the technology, skills and tools available at Sturgis Library at this time. They have helped in coordinating the expertise of both the Technical Services and Public Services to recognize and meet the needs of patrons, who now have more complete and more current access to Sturgis Library's resources available to them from both on and off campus. They have aided in identifying redundant titles in holdings so that appropriate cuts could be made. The dynamic Web pages are widely used by both patrons and staff and have served us well, particularly for several years during the library's transition to a new library automation system, with which staff will soon begin full cataloging of the periodical holdings; and they have laid the groundwork for future development of dynamic Web applications by Sturgis's own library staff.

NOTES

1. Kristin Antelman, "Getting Out of the HTML Business: The Database-Driven Web Site Solution," *Information Technology and Libraries* 18, no. 4 (1999): 176-181.

2. Marshall Breeding, "A Tutorial in Creating Web-Enabled Databases with Inmagic DB/TextWorks Through ODBC," *Library Computing* 19, no. 1/2 (2000): 18-34.

3. Kristin Antelman, Frank Cervone, Andrew Bullen, "Moving Out of HTML into Database Solutions," Internet Librarian '99 Conference, San Diego, California, November 9, 1999.

4. Karl Beiser, "Database-Driven Web Sites," *Database Magazine* 20, no. 6 (1997): 48-52.

5. Karen R. Harker, "Order Out of Chaos," *Library Computing* 18, no. 1 (1999): 59-67.

The Internet Collegiate Reference Collection

William J. Frost

SUMMARY. The parameters of the Internet Collegiate Reference Collection <http://icrc.library.bloomu.edu> closely resemble that of a print collection. It has guidelines for addition and withdrawal of resources and an OPAC, which provides keyword searching through a relational database using open source software. Each entry is assigned a classification code, subject headings, and descriptive notes. *[Article copies available for a fee from The Haworth Document Delivery Service: 1-800-HAWORTH. E-mail address: <getinfo@haworthpressinc.com> Website: <http://www.HaworthPress.com> © 2002 by The Haworth Press, Inc. All rights reserved.]*

KEYWORDS. College and university students, reference collections, Internet resources, database construction, open source software, PHP, PostgreSQL

Imagine a reference collection where a publisher or vendor may recall a title from your shelves without notice and provide no replacement. Other titles disappear as well from their assigned place and reappear in another. When found elsewhere, you must make changes in your OPAC to make the titles once more accessible.

The paragraph above describes, of course, the shortcomings of a collection of free reference sources on the Internet. But the positive aspects

---

William J. Frost (fros@bloomu.edu) is Webmaster/Database Coordinator/Reference Librarian, Harvey A. Andruss Library, Bloomsburg University of Pennsylvania, 400 East 2nd Street, Bloomsburg, PA 17815-1301.

[Haworth co-indexing entry note]: "The Internet Collegiate Reference Collection." Frost, William J. Co-published simultaneously in *Internet Reference Services Quarterly* (The Haworth Information Press, an imprint of The Haworth Press, Inc.) Vol. 7, No. 1/2, 2002, pp. 123-130; and: *Database-Driven Web Sites* (ed: Kristin Antelman) The Haworth Information Press, an imprint of The Haworth Press, Inc., 2002, pp. 123-130. Single or multiple copies of this article are available for a fee from The Haworth Document Delivery Service [1-800-HAWORTH, 9:00 a.m. - 5:00 p.m. (EST). E-mail address: getinfo@haworthpressinc.com].

far outweigh the negative. Links need only a few kilobytes of storage rather than hundreds of feet of shelf space. The free Web sources are often as good as their print counterparts, and they are available to readers at any location. As opposed to a print source, digital references are often searchable by keyword. And they are free! A collection of free online sources complements the print and electronic titles purchased for a library's reference collection.

BEGINNINGS

As did many other libraries in the mid-1990s, the Harvey A. Andruss Library of Bloomsburg University of Pennsylvania added links to the free versions of such standard databases as ERIC, MEDLINE, and Agricola on its HTML Web pages. At first they were integrated with the list of subscription databases. When both subscription and free reference sources became more plentiful, it was decided to separate them. A more complete list of free reference sources for undergraduates was sought, but nothing already in existence was discovered. Many sites had small "ready reference" collections or large collections of links not limited to reference or to the college level, and some college libraries combined free and subscription sources. Since the Andruss Library already had a good start with many links identified, the decision was made to expand these links into a comprehensive list of free reference titles on the Internet. The selection and organization of reference sources would be the library's contribution to the Web community, having no reference titles of its own to share. Titles of interest only to Pennsylvania students were removed to make the list relevant to a wider audience.

During the summer of 2000 the collection was given a name, the Internet Collegiate Reference Collection (ICRC). By summer's end, the ICRC consisted of over 400 links to encyclopedias, dictionaries, directories, databases, and other tools that were of potential use to any English-speaking undergraduate. The links were arranged by the Library of Congress Classification (LCC) system familiar to the largest number of college students. No more than 50 links/page were allowed, so that each page would load quickly in a browser. Each of the dozen or so pages contained an HTML table with a column each for the linked title, a description of the title, and a link to the title's supplier (see Figure 1). An index page connected to all other pages.

By spring of 2001, the ICRC had grown to 600 titles and was becoming unwieldy. Whenever the collection grew, new pages and new links

FIGURE 1

> **Title**: African American Perspectives
>
> **Provider**: U.S. Library of Congress
>
> **Subject Heading/s**: Afro-Americans--History
>
> **LC Class**: E
>
> **Reference Category**: Catalogs
>
> **Description**: *African American Perspectives: Pamphlets from the Daniel A.P. Murray Collection, 1818-1907* is an index in 7 parts to a collection of 351 pamphlets dealing with slavery, abolition, and civil rights.

had to be made. Using a search engine to find information within the several pages was imprecise. The tool used to write the HTML, BBEdit (the author confesses to being a card-carrying member of the Macintosh community), was mounted on computers at home and work, restricting editing of the ICRC to those locations. It was time to place the collection in a database.

CREATING A DATABASE

A database was planned which would hold at least a thousand records, which could be edited from a computer with any platform, and which could be searched in multiple ways. If it was to be used by many others outside the Bloomsburg University community, the database had to sustain several simultaneous hits. Title, title address, supplier, supplier address, description, and subject heading/s were created (see Figure 2).

The ICRC server is a Hewlett Packard Netserver LC 2000 R with an Intel P3-733 MHz chip, 256 MB RAM, and three 18 GB hard drives, set in a RAID 5 array. Open source software is used to support the ICRC server from beginning to end, thereby causing little expense to the library. For at least a year, the server had been operating with Red Hat Linux and an Apache Web server. The PHP 4 scripting language is used as the interface to the PostgreSQL 7.1 database recommended by Red

FIGURE 2

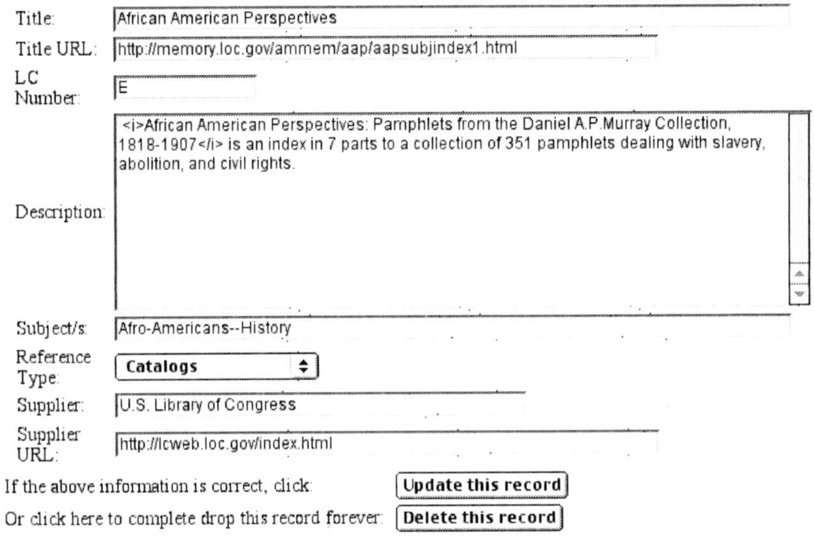

Title:	African American Perspectives
Title URL:	http://memory.loc.gov/ammem/aap/aapsubjindex1.html
LC Number:	E
Description:	*<i>*African American Perspectives: Pamphlets from the Daniel A.P.Murray Collection, 1818-1907*</i>* is an index in 7 parts to a collection of 351 pamphlets dealing with slavery, abolition, and civil rights.
Subject/s:	Afro-Americans--History
Reference Type:	**Catalogs** ⬍
Supplier:	U.S. Library of Congress
Supplier URL:	http://lcweb.loc.gov/index.html

If the above information is correct, click: **[Update this record]**

Or click here to complete drop this record forever: **[Delete this record]**

Hat. A Web-based administrative tool, phpPgAdmin, was found which simplified configuring the PostgreSQL database.

Entries are added, deleted, and changed with forms written in HTML and PHP by William Barnes, the Library Network Administrator, who already knew Perl and similar languages. The author made some changes in the scripts, based on his knowledge of HTML. More about the increasing popularity of PHP and code for various functions may be found on Web sites such as 1 PHP Street <http://www.1phpstreet.com/>.

The experience gained with the ICRC database allowed the library to create similar Postgres databases and PHP scripts. A list of all business and economics periodicals <http://library.bloomu.edu/bpl/> was written for accreditation purposes. One database of the library's microform sets is nearly complete and another for newspaper holdings is under construction.

Student assistants copied the data for each entry from the old ICRC HTML pages and pasted it into forms for the new database. The author then edited each entry. By the end of August 2001, the conversion of the ICRC to a database was complete. Since that time, all data input has been done by the author, who also does all the selection and cataloging.

Editing scripts are password protected, since that process may now be done from any computer with a browser and an Internet connection.

COLLECTION DEVELOPMENT

Internet resources are chosen much the same as books and other media are selected for the Andruss Library's print collections. Additional criteria apply to freely available resources on the Internet, e.g., the type of advertising present.

The ICRC policy (shown below) is found in "About the Collection" page. It is the basis for selection, which is done solely by the author with some helpful suggestions from colleagues and other ICRC users.

ICRC Collection Development Guidelines

- Roughly the same criteria for book selection apply to Web resources as well, e.g., recommendations of reviewers, author's credentials, publisher's/supplier's reputation, inclusion of sources where applicable, currency of data.
- Selection is based upon the contribution of the site to general undergraduate learning for English-speaking students. Although most sources are from the United States, they are not aimed at the needs of any particular institution or geographic location within the U.S.
- Sites are selected for their contribution to undergraduate research and writing, but a few are chosen for students' personal needs.
- Most sites in this collection are specific databases of articles, graphics, statistics, texts, and so forth, where items may be retrieved directly, rather than sites that are portals or menu pages.
- Sites that have data on their servers are preferred to those that link to other sites. Subject lists of Web sites (excepting selected bibliographies or directories) are too numerous and the sites too varied in content to be listed here.
- Content is free, or largely free, and there is no obligation to purchase items when free information is obtained; advertising is not overly intrusive.
- No registration or passwords are required.
- Except for Adobe Reader and the like, the downloading of special software should not be required.

- Digital counterparts of print titles should be accompanied by full citations.
- Links are selective rather than comprehensive. If a title would not be considered for addition to a conventional reference collection, it probably should not be added.
- All sites are visited and searched before being included.
- Links are checked regularly (at least monthly) for changes.

ICRC Collection Development Tools

The identification of some online reference titles is serendipitous, but most are culled from those mentioned in recognized publications and Internet sites. A selected list of selection resources is found below.

- Best Free Reference Web Sites from RUSA Machine-Assisted Reference Section (MARS) <http://www.ala.org/rusa/mars/best2001.html>
- *CHOICE: Current Reviews for Academic Libraries*
- Internet Scout Report <http://scout.cs.wisc.edu/report/sr/current/>
- Librarians' Index to the Internet (LII) <http://lii.org/>
- ResearchBuzz News <http://www.researchbuzz.com/news/>
- Virtual Acquisition Shelf & News Desk from Gary Price <http://resourceshelf.blogspot.com/>

Links in the ICRC are made directly to the reference title, rather than to the site's home page. Some reference sources are buried several layers deep in a site and might be difficult for even experienced searchers to find. They form part of the Invisible Web that many search engines do not penetrate. The ICRC links directly to each title, e.g., the *Columbia Encyclopedia* <http://www.bartleby.com/65/>. It also links to, as well as cites, Bartleby.com <http://www.bartleby.com/> as the supplier of the encyclopedia. The purpose of the supplier link is to facilitate finding a reference title from the supplier's home page if the direct link to the title changes.

It takes approximately one hour to add each title to the ICRC, which includes researching, but then rejecting titles not meeting the above criteria, and assigning classification and subject headings. Cataloging was found to be often as time-consuming for an entry as selection. At least half the titles were added during personal time.

CATALOGING AND CLASSIFICATION

The ICRC uses the Library of Congress Classification (LCC) scheme <http://lcweb.loc.gov/catdir/cpso/lcco/lcco.html>, used by more academic libraries than any other system. Subject headings are likewise those of the Library of Congress.

Descriptions taken from the supplier are used whenever possible and placed in quotes. Input forms and database fields were constructed to accommodate lengthy descriptions. Paragraph and line breaks in the descriptions are hand coded.

ICRC Cataloging and Classification Guidelines

- Classification is taken only to the subclass level, which is the second letter in LCC, e.g., "HG." Classifying beyond that point would have been very time consuming for a relatively small collection of titles that will never be shelved.
- Subject bibliographies are placed with the subject subclass, omitting subclass Z1001-8999. All style manuals are placed in LB.
- The online catalogs of the Harvey A. Andruss Library and the Library of Congress are used as a reference when classification or subject headings are not obvious.

Using the Catalog

Entries may be viewed in two ways: (1) browsing by LC subclass, and (2) keyword searching. All fields except LC classification are searched by keyword, including Internet address fields; thus, a keyword search of ".gov" will bring up all entries provided by government agencies.

Updating and Weeding

Student assistants working in the library's reference unit check for broken links. Using a printout of the Contents by LC Class page, they proceed through the LC subclasses one by one. When finished with the Z's, they start over, much the same as with shelf-reading a print collection. A copy of the page with suspect links is given to the author for further checking and possible editing. Approximately two hours per week of student time is used for checking links.

Any address that does not link after a week's time is a candidate for withdrawal. In some cases, Webmasters of a site have been contacted to determine the fate of a particularly useful title. The End of Free <http://www.theendoffree.com/> is checked periodically to determine if free reference sources have changed status.

USAGE

There is little at this time in the way of usage statistics for the ICRC, but there are plans to develop ways of supplying them. To facilitate statistical accounting, the collection was recently assigned a site address, <http://icrc.bloomu.edu>, rather than the former directory address, <http://library.bloomu.edu/library/reference/>. Some thought has also been given to gauge user satisfaction, since there is currently nothing now but the enthusiastic support of Bloomsburg University reference librarians and some external users to indicate value.

CONCLUSION

With a selection policy aimed at a specific clientele, partial cataloging, and with an OPAC having both subject and keyword access, the Internet Collegiate Reference Collection is unique in being a virtual collection that so closely approximates an actual collection of undergraduate reference resources. The ICRC is now easier both to use and to maintain; there are no more pages of HTML to edit and no more FTP transactions to make.

Libraries that continue to provide hundreds of links to Internet resources may wish to put them in a database and give them brief classification for increased ease of maintenance and use. Those who find it expedient to use the ICRC as their catalog of free reference titles are more than welcome to do so. The collection now numbers over 850 titles. As a work in progress, readers' suggestions for the ICRC are welcome.

Index